anarchism

a beginner's guide

anarchism

a beginner's guide

ruth kinna

ONEWORLD
OXFORD

anarchism: a beginner's guide

Oneworld Publications
(Sales and Editorial)
185 Banbury Road
Oxford OX2 7AR
England
www.oneworld-publications.com

ISBN-13: 978–1–85168–370–3
ISBN-10: 1–85168–370–4

Typeset by Jayvee, Trivandrum, India
Cover design by the Bridgewater Book Company
Printed and bound by WS Bookwell, Finland

contents

acknowledgements

A number of people have helped in the production of this book. Many thanks to Sharif Gemie and Vasilis Margaras for reading and commenting on early drafts, and to Dave Berry for generously giving his time to share his extensive knowledge of anarchist labour history – as well as lending some valuable materials. Thanks also to Simon Tormey who read and offered helpful comments on the original manuscript. Sadly, none of them have managed to iron out all the creases, but I'm very grateful for their help and encouragement. The production team at Oneworld – especially Victoria Roddam, who suggested the project, Mark Hopwood and Judy Kearns – have been extremely helpful and I'm grateful for their responsiveness and patience in seeing the book through.

Finally, I'd like to thank family and friends – some I didn't know I had – who helped out in the dark days of 2002–3 and especially to Robert and Andrew who bore the brunt of those times. This book is for them.

introduction

This book falls into four chapters, each organized around a particular theme: (i) the ideology of anarchism; (ii) anarchist conceptions
of the state; (iii) principles of anarchist organization (ideas of
anarchy); and (iv) strategies for change.

The first chapter begins by introducing the terms 'anarchism',
'anarchist' and 'anarchy' and then discusses the problems anarchists
have encountered with popular conceptions of anarchy. The main
body of the chapter looks at three different approaches to anarchism.
The first seeks to understand the core principles of anarchism by
abstracting key ideas from the works of designated anarchist
thinkers. The second emphasizes the broadness of the ideology by
categorizing anarchists into a variety of schools or traditions. The
third approach is historical and argues that anarchism developed in
response to a peculiar set of political circumstances, active in the
latter decades of nineteenth-century Europe. The aim of this chapter
is to suggest that anarchism can be defined as an ideology by the
adherence of anarchists to a core belief namely, the rejection of the
state.

The second chapter considers some of the ways in which
anarchists have theorized the state and the grounds on which they
have called for its abolition. It looks in particular at anarchist ideas
of government, authority and power and it uses these ideas to show
why anarchists believe the state to be both detrimental and unnecessary. Anarchists sometimes suggest that they are wholly opposed to
government, authority and power, but the chapter shows how these
concepts are incorporated into anarchist theories to bolster
anarchist defences of anarchy. Finally, the chapter reviews some

1

anarchist theories of liberty, in an effort to show why anarchists believe anarchy is superior to the state, and to illustrate the broad difference between anarchist communitarians and libertarians.

The third chapter looks at anarchist ideas of organization and some models of anarchy. It looks first at the ways in which anarchists have understood the relationship between anarchy and statelessness, and the use they have made of anthropology to formulate ideas of anarchy. The second part of the chapter considers anarchist responses to utopianism, identifies decentralized federalism as the principle of anarchist planning and outlines two 'utopian' views of this principle. The final part of the chapter considers some experiments in anarchy, both historical and contemporary, highlighting the relationship that some anarchists posit between organization and revolutionary change.

The final chapter examines strategies for change – both revolutionary and evolutionary – and different methods of protest, from symbolic to direct action. The chapter includes a discussion of anarchist responses to the anti-globalization movement and reviews one of the important arguments that anti-globalization protest has raised: the justification of violence.

what is anarchism?

There cannot *be a history of anarchism in the sense of establishing a permanent state of things called 'anarchist'. It is always a continual coping with the next situation, and a vigilance to make sure that past freedoms are not lost and do not turn into the opposite ...*

(Paul Goodman, in *A Decade of Anarchy*, p. 39)

What do we anarchists believe? ... we believe that human beings can achieve their maximum development and fulfilment as individuals in a community of individuals only when they have free access to the means of life and are equals among equals, we maintain that to achieve a society in which these conditions are possible it is necessary to destroy all that is authoritarian in existing society.

(Vernon Richards, *Protest Without Illusions*, p. 129)

Anarchism is a doctrine that aims at the liberation of peoples from political domination and economic exploitation by the encouragement of direct or non-governmental action. Historically, it has been linked to working-class activism, but its intellectual roots lie in the mid-nineteenth century, just prior to the era of mass organization. Europe was anarchism's first geographical centre, and the early decades of the twentieth century marked the period of its greatest success. Yet the influence of anarchism has extended across the globe, from America to China; whilst anarchism virtually disappeared after 1939, when General Franco crushed the Spanish revolution to end the civil war, today it is again possible to talk about an anarchist movement or movements. The origins of contemporary anarchism can be traced to 1968 when, to the delight and surprise of activists – and disappointment and incredulity of critics – student rebellion put anarchism back on the political agenda. There is some dispute in anarchist circles about the character and composition of the late-twentieth and twenty-first-century anarchism and its relationship to the earlier twentieth-century movement. But all agree that anarchism has been revived and there is some optimism that anarchist ideas are again exercising a real influence in contemporary politics. This influence is detectable in numerous campaigns – from highly publicized protests against animal vivisection, millitarization and nuclear arms, to less well-known programmes for urban renewal, the development of alternative media, free education, radical democracy and co-operative labour. Anarchist ideas have also made themselves felt in the anti-capitalist, anti-globalization movement – sometimes dubbed by activists as the pro-globlization movement or the movement for globalization from below.

Anarchists are those who work to further the cause of anarchism. Like activists in other movements, those who struggle in the name of anarchism fall into a number of categories ranging from educationalists and propagandists to combatants in armed struggle. Anarchists work in local and international arenas, building networks for community action and showing solidarity with comrades locked in struggles in areas like Palestine and the Chiapas region of Mexico.

Because anarchists eschew party politics, their diversity is perhaps more apparent than it is in other organizations. The development of discrete anarchist schools of thought will be examined in some detail later on in the chapter. But as a starting point, it is useful to indicate three areas of difference to help to distinguish the concerns of contemporary anarchists. Some of those calling themselves anarchist consider anarchism to be a political movement directed towards the liberation of the working class. In the past, this struggle was centred on urban industrial workers, though in places like Spain it also embraced rural workers. Today, anarchists in this group also make appeals to women and people of colour within the working class and combine their traditional concern to overcome economic oppression with an interest to combat racism, sexism and fascism. Anarchists in this band include groups affiliated to the International Workers' Association (IWA): the Solidarity Federation in Britain and the Confederación Nacional del Trabajo (CNT) in Spain. In contrast, other anarchists see anarchism as a vast umbrella movement, importantly radicalized by feminists, ecologists, gays and lesbians. Anarchists in this group, often suspicious of being categorized by any *ism*, tend to see anarchism as a way of life or a collective commitment to a counter-cultural lifestyle defined by interdependence and mutual support. Variations of this idea are expressed by anarchists linked to the journal *Social Anarchism* as well as by European 'insurrectionists' like Alfredo Bonanno. A third group similarly downplays the idea of working-class struggle to emphasize the aesthetic dimension of liberation, building on an association with art that has its roots in the nineteenth century. For these anarchists, anarchism is a revolutionary movement directed towards the need to overcome the alienation, boredom and consumerism of everyday life. Its essence lies in challenging the system through cultural subversion, creating confusion to highlight the oppressiveness of accepted norms and values. Anarchists in this group include self-styled anti-anarchist anarchists like Bob Black and primitivists like John Moore.

Anarchy is the goal of anarchists: the society variously described to be without government or without authority; a condition of statelessness, of free federation, of 'complete' freedom and equality based either on rational self-interest, co-operation or reciprocity. Though there are fewer conceptions of anarchy than there are anarchists, the anarchist ideal has been conceptualized in a variety of ways. What holds them together is the idea that anarchy is an ordered way of life. Indeed, the origin of the familiar graffiti – the 'A' in a circle – derives from the slogan 'Anarchy is order; government is civil war', coined by Pierre-Joseph Proudhon in 1848 and symbolized by the revolutionary Anselme Bellegarrigue. Notwithstanding the regularity with which Bellegarrigue's graffiti appears on bus shelters and railway lines, anarchists have not been able to communicate their ideas very effectively and, instead of being accepted as a term that describes a possible set of futures, anarchy is usually taken to denote a condition of chaos, disorder and disruption. Indeed, 'anarchy' was already being used in this second sense before anarchists like Proudhon adopted it to describe their ideal. Whilst studies of the origins of the word 'anarchy' are part and parcel of most introductions to anarchist thought, this well-trodden territory helps to explain the difficulty anarchists have had in defining their position. As G.D.H. Cole noted, 'the Anarchists ... were anarchists because they did not believe in an anarchical world'.[1] Common language, however, has always suggested otherwise.

anarchy: origins of the word

Anarchism is an unusual ideology because its adopted tag has peculiarly negative connotations. Most ideological labels embrace positively valued ideas or ideals: liberalism is the ideology of liberty or freedom, socialism is associated with notions of sociability or fellowship, and conservatism with the conservation of established or customary ways of life. Even fascism has a positive derivation – from *fascio*, a reference to the symbol of Roman authority. In contrast, anarchism is the ideology of anarchy – a term that has been understood in both the history of ideas and in popular culture to imply the breakdown of order, if not violent disorder. Even after the mid-nineteenth century when the label was first adopted as an affirmation of belief, anarchy was used in political debate to ridicule or denounce ideas perceived to be injurious or dangerous. For example, in a seventeenth-century defence of absolute monarchy, Sir Robert Filmer treated calls for limited monarchy as calls for anarchy. In general usage the term is commonly used to describe fear and dread. The 'great Anarch!' in Alexander Pope's *The Dying Christian to his Soul* is the 'dread empire, Chaos!' that brings 'universal darkness' to bury all. The eighteenth-century philosopher Edmund Burke considered anarchy as the likely outcome of the brewing American conflict and identified freedom as its cure. From his rather different political perspective, the poet Percy Bysshe Shelley drew on 'anarchy' to describe the violent duplicity of government, yet like Burke he still conceived the term in a wholly negative sense to describe disorder and injustice. Writing in the nineteenth century, the social critic John Ruskin aptly captured the common view: '[g]overnment and co-operation are in all things the laws of life; anarchy and competition the laws of death'. This conception was the very reverse of Proudhon's.

The anarchist idea of anarchy has its roots in a critique of revolutionary government advanced in the course of the French Revolution. In 1792, a group of revolutionaries known as the *enragés* (the fanatics), because of the zeal with which they entered into their campaigns, demanded that the Jacobin government introduce draconian measures to protect the artisans of Paris from profiteers. Banded around Jacques Roux, an ex-cleric, and Jean Varlet, a man of independent means, the group did not call themselves anarchists. Yet their programme (a call to the people to take direct action against profiteers and the demand that the government provide work and bread), was labelled anarchist by their Jacobin opponents.[2] During their battle with the Jacobins, moreover, Varlet and Roux rejected the idea of revolutionary government as a contradiction in terms, importantly associating anarchism with the rejection of revolution by decree. As the revolution ran its course the revolutionary government continued to apply the term 'anarchist' as a term of political abuse and to discredit those political programmes of which it disapproved. Nevertheless, the idea that anarchy could be used in a positive sense and that anarchism described a political programme was now firmly established. The first four editions of the *Dictionary of the French Academy* (1694–1762) defined anarchy as an unruly condition, without leadership or any sort of government. The exemplification was taken from classical philosophy: 'democracy can easily degenerate into anarchy'. In the fifth edition (1798) the definition of anarchy remained the same, but it was supplemented for the first time with an entry for 'anarchist' that distinguished 'a supporter of anarchy' from 'a trouble-maker'. It was now possible to speak of 'anarchist principles' and an 'anarchist system'.[3]

The revolutionary movement created by the *enragés* left its legacy in the history of ideas. Less than 100 years after the outbreak of revolution, the association between anarchy and the idea of popular revolution inspired the French writer Pierre-Joseph Proudhon to label himself an anarchist. In his first book, *What Is Property?* (1840, where he famously coined the phrase 'property is theft') he appropriated the term anarchy to define his egalitarian and libertarian ideal. Proudhon introduced the term in the following dialogue:

> What is to be the form of government in the future? I hear some of my younger readers reply: 'Why, how can you ask such a question? You are a republican!' 'A republican! Yes; but that word specifies nothing. *Res publica*; that is, the public thing. Now, whoever is interested in public affairs – no matter under what form of government – may call himself a republican. Even kings are republicans.' – 'Well! You are a democrat?' – 'No.' – 'What! you would have a monarchy?' – 'God forbid!' – 'You are then an aristocrat?' – 'Not at all.' – 'You want a mixed government?' – 'Still less.' – 'What are you, then?' – 'I am an anarchist.'
>
> 'Oh! I understand you; you speak satirically. This is a hit at the government.' – 'By no means. I have just given you my serious and

well considered profession of faith. Although a firm friend of order, I am (in the full force of the term) an anarchist. ....'[4]

As George Woodcock noted, Proudhon delighted in paradox and fully appreciated the ambiguity of the term 'anarchy' when he adopted it to describe his politics. Tracing the origin of the word to the ancient Greek (*anarkhos*) he argued that anarchy meant 'without government', or the government of no one. Far from implying social ruin, it suggested progress and harmonious co-operation. Anarchy was the natural counterpart to equality: it promised an end to social division and civil strife. In the nineteenth century some anarchists inserted a hyphen between the 'an' and 'archy', in an effort to emphasize its derivation from antiquity, whilst also drawing implicit comparison with the better-known alternatives, monarchy (the government of one), and oligarchy (the government of the few). By hyphenating the word in this manner they hoped to challenge their detractors whilst encouraging the oppressed to re-examine their ideas about the nature of political organization and the assumptions on which these ideas were based.

Some anarchists have shared Proudhon's delight in the paradox of 'anarchy' and played up the positive aspect of chaos associated with the term. The Russian anarchist Michael Bakunin famously described the disordered order of anarchy in the revolutionary principle: 'the passion for destruction is a creative passion, too'.[5] Another nineteenth-century Russian, Peter Kropotkin, followed suit. Order, he argued, was 'servitude ... the shackling of thought, the brutalizing of the human race, maintained by the sword and the whip.' Disorder was 'the uprising of the people against this ignoble order, breaking its fetters, destroying the barriers, and marching towards a better future.' Of course anarchy spelt disorder for it promised 'the blossoming of the most beautiful passions and the greatest of devotion': it was 'the epic of supreme human love'.[6] Other anarchists have been less comfortable with the connotations of 'anarchy'. Indeed, much anarchist literature suggests that the ambiguity of 'anarchy' has forced anarchists onto the defensive. As many anarchists have pointed out, the problem of Proudhon's paradox is not only the confusion to which it lends itself, but its broadness: disorder can imply anything from disorganization to barbarism and violence. One of the most persistent features of introductions to anarchism is the author's concern to demythologize this idea. Examples from three different authors are reproduced below. The first is taken from

Alexander Berkman's *ABC of Anarchism*:

> ... before I tell you what anarchism is, I want to tell you what it *is not*.
> That is necessary because so much falsehood has been spread about
> anarchism. Even intelligent persons often have entirely wrong
> notions about it. Some people talk about anarchism without
> knowing a thing about it. And some lie about anarchism, because
> they don't want you to know the truth about it. ...
> Therefore I must tell you, first of all, what anarchism is *not*.
> It is *not* bombs, disorder, or chaos.
> It is *not* robbery and murder.
> It is *not* a war of each against all.
> It is *not* a return to barbarism or to the wild state of man.
> *Anarchism is the very opposite of all that.*[7]

The second comes from the Cardiff-based Anarchist Media Group:

> There is probably more rubbish talked about anarchism than any
> other political idea. Actually it has nothing to do with a belief in
> chaos, death and destruction. Anarchists do not normally carry
> bombs, nor do they ascribe any virtue to beating up old ladies ...
> ... There is nothing complicated or threatening about anarchism ...[8]

Finally, Donald Rooum offers this in his introduction to anarchism:

> Besides being used in the sense implied by its Greek origin, the word
> 'anarchy' is also used to mean unsettled government, disorderly
> government, or government by marauding gangs ...
> Both the proper and improper meanings of the term 'anarchy' are
> now current, and this causes confusion. A person who hears gov-
> ernment by marauding gangs described as 'anarchy' on television
> news, and then hears an anarchist advocating 'anarchy', is liable to
> conclude that anarchists want government by marauding gangs.[9]

Of course, anarchists have moved beyond these disclaimers to
advance fairly detailed conceptions of anarchy and to highlight the
success that anarchy has enjoyed, albeit on a temporary and pro-
scribed scale. Yet anarchy remains a problematic concept because,
unlike liberty for example, it so readily lends itself to the evocation of
an unattractive condition. And whilst anarchists are happy to discuss
the possibility of moving beyond existing forms of state organization
they have been wary of employing 'anarchy' as an explanatory concept, preferring to define anarchism in other ways. The remainder of

the chapter examines three alternative approaches to anarchism: the first looks at key personalities, the second at schools of thought and the third at history.

anarchist thought: key personalities

One popular approach to the study of anarchism is to trace a history of anarchist ideas through the analysis of key texts or the writings of important thinkers. Paul Eltzbacher, a German judge and scholar, was amongst the first to adopt this approach. His 1900 German-language *Der Anarchismus* identified seven 'sages' of anarchism: joining Proudhon were William Godwin (1756–1836), Max Stirner (1806–1856), Michael Bakunin (1814–1870), Peter Kropotkin (1842–1921), Benjamin Tucker (1854–1939) and Leo Tolstoy (1828–1910). Eltzbacher's list has rarely been treated as definitive, though George Woodcock's *Anarchism* (1962), which remains a standard reference work, largely followed Eltzbacher's selection, dropping only Tucker from special consideration in the family of key thinkers. Nevertheless, Eltzbacher's approach remains popular. Its discussion both provides an introduction to some of the characters whose work will be examined during the course of this book and, perhaps more importantly, raises an on-going debate about the possibility of defining anarchism by a unifying idea.

Arguments about who should be included in the anarchist canon usually turn on assessments of the influence that writers have exercised on the movement and tend to reflect particular cultural, historical and political biases of the selector. For example, in Anglo-American studies, Bakunin and Kropotkin are normally represented as the most important anarchist theorists; in Continental Europe, especially in France, Proudhon and Bakunin are more likely to be identified as the movement's leading lights. In recent years selectors have tended to widen the net of those considered to be at the forefront of anarchist thought. In *Demanding the Impossible* (1992), Peter Marshall not only restored Tucker to the canon, he expanded it to include Elisée Reclus (1830–1905), Errico Malatesta (1853–1932) and Emma Goldman (1869–1940). The same tendency is apparent in anthologies of anarchist writings. Daniel Guérin's collection, *No Gods, No Masters*, makes no reference to Godwin, Tucker or Tolstoy but includes work by Casar de Paepe (1842–90), James Guillaume (1844–1916), Malatesta, Ferdinand Pelloutier

(1867–1901) and Emile Pouget (1860–1931), Voline (the pseudo-nym of Vsevolod Mikhailovich Eichenbaum, 1882–1945) and Nestor Makhno (1889–1935). George Woodcock's *Anarchist Reader* shows a similar diversity, though it leans far more towards the North American tradition than Guérin's collection and also includes twentieth-century figures like Rudolf Rocker (1873–1958), Murray Bookchin (b. 1921), Herbert Read (1893–1968), Alex Comfort (1920–2000), Nicholas Walter (1934–2000), Colin Ward (b. 1924) and Paul Goodman (1911–1972).

The popularity of Eltzbacher's approach owes something to Kropotkin – one of his subjects – who in 1910 endorsed Eltzbacher's study as 'the best work on Anarchism'.[10] One measure of the method's success is the distinction that is now commonly drawn between the 'classical' theoreticians of anarchism, and the rest. This distinction is particularly marked in academic work. Even whilst nominating different candidates to the rank of classical theorist, by and large academics treat nineteenth-century anarchists as a body of writers who raised anarchism to 'a level of articulation that distin-guished it as a serious political theory' and disregard the remainder as mere agitators and propagandists.[11] In a less than hearty endorse-ment of anarchism, George Crowder maintained that the '"great names" are indeed relatively great because their work was more ori-ginal, forceful and influential than that of others'.[12] Some writers from within – or close to – the anarchist movement have also supported the idea of a classical tradition. Daniel Guérin's guide to anarchism, *No Gods, No Masters*, includes only writings from those judged to be in the first rank of anarchist thought. The contribution of 'their second-rate epigones' is duly dismissed.[13] A similar distinc-tion is maintained in popular anarchist publications. Pamphlets and broadsheets produced by anarchist groups continue to focus on the work of Makhno, Kropotkin, Bakunin and Malatesta; and reprints of original work by this intellectual elite can be readily found at anarchist book-fairs and on websites. Some activists are also happy to publish as anarchist literature the work of leading academic social critics – notably Noam Chomsky – establishing a new tier to the intellectual hierarchy.

Yet Eltzbacher's method has not been accepted without criticism. Indeed, its success has prompted a good deal of debate and his approach has been attacked on a number of grounds. As Guérin noted, one problem with Eltzbacher's approach is that it can tend towards biography and away from the analysis of ideas. When the work of the masters is given less priority than the details of their lives, the danger is that the meaning of anarchism can be muddled by the tendency of leading anarchists to act inconsistently or some- times in contradiction to their stated beliefs.[14] Another problem is the apparent arbitrariness of Eltzbacher's selection. Here, com- plaints tend in opposite directions. Some have argued that the canon is too inclusive, composed of fellow travellers who never called themselves anarchists and those who adopted the tag without show- ing any real commitment to the movement. Others suggest that the approach is too exclusive and that it disregards the contribution of the numberless, nameless activists who have kept the anarchist movement alive.

The problem of inclusion has been exacerbated by the habit of some writers to treat anarchism as a tendency apparent in virtually all schools of political thought. Armed with a broad conception of anarchism as a belief in the possibility of society without govern- ment, anarchists from Kropotkin to Herbert Read have pointed to everything from ancient Chinese philosophy, Zoroastrianism and early Christian thought as sources of anarchism. The father of Taoism, Lao Tzu, the sixteenth-century essayist Etienne de la Boetie, the French encyclopaedist Denis Diderot, the American Transcendentalist David Henry Thoreau, Fydor Dostoyevsky and Oscar Wilde, and political leaders like Mohandas Gandhi, have all been included in anthologies or histories of anarchism. As Nicolas Walter argued, this inclusiveness can be misleading:

> The description of a past golden age without government may be found in the thought of ancient China and India, Egypt and Mesopotamia, and Greece and Rome, and in the same way the wish for a future utopia without government may be found in the thought of countless religious and political writers and commu- nities. But the application of anarchy to the present situation is more recent, and it is only in the anarchist movement of the nineteenth century that we find the demand for a society without government here and now.[15]

The reverse complaint, that the canon is too exclusive, is in part a protest about the restrictedness of the choices. Who decides which anarchists have made the most important contribution to anarchist thought or to history? In his account of the German anarchist movement Andrew Carlson criticizes theorists of anarchism like

Eltzbacher for wrongly suggesting that the German movement produced no writers of repute and that anarchist ideas exercised only a
marginal influence on the German socialist movement.[16] Neither
view is supportable. Equally misleading is the view, sustained by the
canon, that women have made little contribution to anarchism. The
anarchist movement has boasted a number of women activists, apart
from Emma Goldman, including Louise Michel (1830–1905), Lucy
Parsons (1853–1942), Charlotte Wilson (1854–1944) and Voltairine
de Cleyre (1866–1912). These women have made a significant
contribution to anarchism and their exclusion from the canon is a
sign of unreasonable neglect.

In the other part, the complaints about exclusivity touch on the
abstraction involved in the process of selection. Many anarchists
resent the way in which the study of anarchist thought has been
divorced from the political context in which the theory was first
advanced. Such a distinction, they argue, legitimizes the intense
scrutiny of a tiny volume of anarchist writings and encourages the
achievements of the wider movement to be overlooked or ignored.
Some anarchists, it's true, have worked hard to elaborate a coherent
anarchist world view: Kropotkin made a self-conscious effort to present himself as a philosopher. But even Kropotkin recognized that
anarchism was defined by the countless newspapers and pamphlets
that circulated in working-class circles, not by the theories spawned
by people like himself. The vast majority of anarchists have worked as
essayists and propagandists and it seems unreasonable and unneces-
sarily restrictive to assess anarchism through the examination of a
tiny, unrepresentative sample of literature. The point is made by
Kingsley Widmer:

> The parochialism of thinking of anarchism generally just in the
> Baukunin-Kropotkin [sic] nineteenth-century matrix, even when
> adding, say, Stirner, Thoreau, Tolstoy or ... what turned-you-on-in-
> a-libertarian-way, just won't do – not only in ideas but in sensibility,
> not only in history but in possibility ... Either anarchism should be
> responded to as various and protean, or it is the mere pathos of
> defeats and the marginalia of political theory.[17]

Leaving the problem of arbitrariness aside, other critics have
directed their fire at the conclusions Eltzbacher drew from his study.
At the end of his book, Eltzbacher attempted to distil from the wide
and disparate body of work he surveyed a unifying idea or core
belief that would serve to define anarchism. The idea he settled upon

was – as the French Academy suggested – the rejection of the state. Anarchists, Eltzbacher famously argued, 'negate the State for our future'.[18] In all the other areas Eltzbacher pinpointed – law, property, political change and statelessness – anarchists were divided. The controversy generated by this conclusion has centred on two points. For some critics Eltzbacher was right to identify anarchism with the rejection of the state, but mistaken in his attempt to classify anarchist families of thought by an apparently scientific method which imposed on anarchism concepts – of property, the state and so forth – that were drawn from legal theory. As one critic put the point, Eltzbacher's 'analysis and presentation possessed the finality of a court judgement'. Other critics have been more concerned with Eltzbacher's general conclusion than with the means by which he purported to distinguish schools of anarchist thought. From this point of view, his mistake was the attempt to identify a common thread in anarchism. Marie Fleming has forcefully advanced the case. In her study of Elisée Reclus – a writer conspicuous by his absence from Eltzbacher's study – Fleming argues that the study of sages imposes a putative, yet meaningless, unity of tradition on a set of ideas that are not only diverse but also often incompatible. As she points out, Eltzbacher himself admitted that his defining principle – the rejection of the state – was filled with 'totally different meanings'. In his insistence that anarchists be drawn together in one school of thought, he wrongly prioritized philosophy over history. He encouraged the idea that 'anarchism embodied a peculiar way of looking at the world' and overlooked the extent to which it was 'a movement that ... developed in response to specific social-economic grievances in given historical circumstances'.[19]

Fleming's criticism of Eltzbacher's method is important but it has not undermined the appeal of classical anarchism and should not be taken as a rebuttal of Eltzbacher's leading conclusion that anarchism implies a rejection of the state. Individual anarchists will of course continue to centre their anarchism on a range of different concepts – usually more positive than the state's rejection. Nevertheless the rejection of the state is a useful ideological marker and one that resonates in popular culture. Moreover, it's possible to find a corrective for the general unease created by Eltzbacher's legalism in two alternative methods of analysis. The first seeks to understand anarchism by distinguishing between different schools of thought. The second is based on a historical analysis of the anarchist movement. These approaches shed a more subtle light than

Eltzbacher was able to do on the nature of anarchist anti-statism. Specifically, the analysis of schools has helped to illustrate the broadness of this concept, and the historical approach its relationship to anti-capitalism.

anarchist thought: schools of anarchism

Anarchists have appended a dizzying array of prefixes and suffixes to 'anarchism' to describe their particular beliefs. Anarchism has been packaged in anarcho-syndicalist, anarcha-feminist, eco-anarchist and anarcho-communist, Christian, social, anarcho-capitalist, reformist and primitivist varieties.

Some anarchists treat these divisions lightly. One doubting sympathizer, the writer Harold Barclay, dubs himself an anarcho-cynicalist. Others find them more problematic. Some dismiss the seemingly endless subdivision of anarchism on the grounds that the labels are excessively sectarian and that they obscure the important bonds that exist between different groups. Others have been fearful that the divisions conceal an un-anarchist intolerance towards others. In the 1880s the Spanish anarchist Ricardo Mella called for an anarchism 'pure and simple', 'anarchism without adjectives' in an effort to avoid straight-jacketing the aspirations of the oppressed in a post-revolutionary situation.[20] Voltairine de Cleyre endorsed Mella's position. Since '[l]iberty and experiment alone can determine the best forms of society' she called herself "[a]narchist" simply'. Taking the different tack, some anarchists have argued that the division of anarchists into schools exaggerates the insignificant differences between anarchists whilst blurring the really significant ones. For example, Voltairine de Cleyre mapped her anarchism pure and simple onto a distinction between anarchism 'old' and 'young', where the old were those who had lost their enthusiasm for the cause, and the young were the often quite elderly comrades who continued to live 'with the faith of hope'.[21] Writing from a rather different perspective John Moore invoked a similar distinction. Finding the existing '57 varieties' of anarchism un-edifying, he encouraged anarchists to adopt a new bi-polar categorization which distinguished the minimalist, reformist, nostalgic 'politics of "if only ..."' from the maximalist, revolutionary, dynamic 'anti-politics of "[w]hat if ...?"'.[22]

Yet for all these complaints, anarchists continue to identify themselves by their particular affiliations and beliefs. In response to the

question 'Who are the anarchists? What do they believe?' six inter-
viewees for a 1968 BBC radio programme responded:

> I consider myself to be an anarchist-communist, in the Kropotkin
> tradition.
>   I think ... I would say I was an anarchist-socialist, or libertarian
> socialist ...
>   I would describe myself as an anarcho-syndicalist ...
>   I don't call myself an anarcho-syndicalist. I could be called an
> anarcho-pacifist-individualist with slight communist tendencies ...
>   I'm an anarchist ... and also think that syndicalism is the anarchist
> application to organising industry.
>   I describe myself as a Stirnerite, a conscious egoist.[23]

The remainder of this chapter will consider what these and other
labels mean, and the relationship between anarchist schools. It
begins with a review of some of the traditional typologies and then
considers the development of some modern schools. At the end of
the chapter, I consider what light the discussion of typology
sheds on Eltzbacher's definition of anarchism as the rejection of
the state.

The subdivision of anarchists into discrete schools began in the
nineteenth century. At first anarchists tended to group themselves
into one of two main schools: communist and non-communist. For
example, in 1894 the English writer Henry Seymour identified two
types of anarchism, one he called mutualistic and the other commun-
istic. Seymour argued that these two doctrines were based on
incompatible economic and social principles. The idea of mutualism
was to ensure that all workers enjoyed an equal right to land and the
means of production, and that monopoly – in the form of rent,
interest, profit and taxation – was abolished. Mutualism also
encouraged competition between producers, in accordance with the
laws of the market. In mutualism, free producers would contract
with one another and a special Bank of Exchange would advance
credit and help facilitate exchanges between them. In anarcho-
communism, by contrast, the community would control property,
and the means of production and individuals would be equalized in
terms of their comforts rather than their rights. There would be no
market exchange. Instead, communists encouraged co-operation
and mutual support. Whereas the principle of mutualism was 'the
product to the producer and each according to his deeds', the idea of

communism was 'the product to the community and each according
to his needs'. In the social sphere, Seymour argued, the differences
between the two doctrines were equally stark. Both mutualism
and communism supported free love. But whereas mutualism
supported marriage and the family (so long as it was based on the
equal liberty and mutual responsibility of the contracting parties),
communism challenged both institutions. In particular, communists charged the community with the care of children, not the
biological parents, and it thereby encouraged the abandonment of
social propriety.[24]

Voltairine de Cleyre followed a similar system of classification,
but instead of distinguishing anarcho-communism from mutualism, she labelled the competing position individualism. Anarchism,
she argued, is

> ... [a] sort of Protestantism, whose adherents are a unit in the great
> essential belief that all forms of external authority must disappear to
> be replaced by self-control only, but variously divided in our con-
> ception for the form of future society. Individualism supposes pri-
> vate property to be the cornerstone of personal freedom; asserts that
> such property should consist in the absolute possession of one's
> own product and of such share of the natural heritage of all as one
> may actually use. Communist-Anarchism, on the other hand,
> declares that such property is both unrealisable and undesirable;
> that the common possession and use of all the natural sources and
> means of social production can alone guarantee the individuals
> against a recurrence of inequality and its attendants, government
> and slavery.[25]

In his 1905 entry for 'anarchism' in the *Encyclopaedia Britannica*
Peter Kropotkin expanded these typologies to distinguish six
main schools of thought: mutualist, individualist, collectivist (also
known as federalist or anti-authoritarian), communist (to which
he aligned himself), Christian and literary. Kropotkin's complex
scheme was based on the consideration of ethical as well as
economic criteria. For example, following Seymour, he agreed that
mutualists and communists differed in their approach to the
market, but he embellished his definition of anarcho-communism
by identifying it with the moral principle: 'do as you would be
done by'. Pursuing a similar line of thought Kropotkin described
individualism as the demand for the 'full liberation of the individual

from all social and moral bonds'. Individualist anarchists dreamed of the creation of a society of egotists. Theirs was a doctrine of 'complete "a-moralism"' and their ethic was 'mind your own business'.

Kropotkin argued that collectivism was closely aligned with communism and that it shared the same morality. Yet collectivism was particularly associated with the demand that state organization be replaced by a system of decentralized federation constructed through the free agreement of autonomous communities. Collectivism suggested that each collective in the federation would own its own property and the means of production – the land, machinery and so forth used to produce goods and services. It also suggested that each collective would be able to decide how goods and services would be distributed to individual members. This was a confusing idea, as Kropotkin recognized, since collectivism was usually understood by non-anarchist socialists to imply the principle of 'distribution according to work' – i.e. a system of individual, differential reward. However, Kropotkin's controversial view was that anarchist collectivism need not necessarily describe a collectivist system in this sense and that it was possible within the federal framework for collectivists to adopt the communist principle of distribution according to need.

Christian anarchism, as the name suggested, took its lead from Biblical teachings and was associated with an idea of fellowship and individual moral regeneration. Notwithstanding its religious foundation, Kropotkin believed that its vision of Christian fellowship dovetailed with anarcho-communism and that its moral principles could as easily be derived from reason as from God. Kropotkin's final school, literary anarchism, was by his own admission hardly a school at all, but a collection of intellectuals and artists – including J.S. Mill, Richard Wagner and Heinrich Ibsen – whose outpourings illustrated the receptiveness of the cultural elite to anarchist ideas. In other words, literary anarchism was an indication of the interpenetration of anarchist ideas with advanced thought.[26]

Subsequent writers have considerably extended and modified Kropotkin's classification. Rudolf Rocker represented anarchism as an evolutionary system of thought. Whilst he accepted Kropotkin's idea that anarchist schools were based, at least in part, on a range of different 'economic assumptions as to the means of safeguarding a free community', he also suggested that they collectively described a progressive movement in thinking. Tracing the evolution of anarchism, he believed that there had been a shift from individualism to collectivism and communism culminating in yet another school of thought: anarcho-syndicalism. This school inherited from collectivism and communism a concern to liberate industrial and rural workers from economic exploitation. What was distinctive about anarcho-syndicalism is that it linked the workers' struggle directly to post-revolutionary organization. Co-operating in unions, or syndicates, workers were organized both to fight against employers and to develop the skills required for them to assume direct control of their factories, workshops and land. In other words, syndicalist – or union – organizations were intended to provide a framework for anarchy.[27]

Aligning himself more closely to Kropotkin than Rocker, Nicolas Walter preferred to see the schools of thought as alternatives rather than aspects of a single idea. However, he questioned Kropotkin's inclusion of individualism (or what he called libertarianism) in anarchism and added syndicalism and another new category – philosophical anarchism – to Kropotkin's original list. This category, Walter argued, appeared in the 1840s, but its most famous modern statement is Robert Paul Wolff's *In Defense of Anarchism*. Wolff's version purported to provide a 'pure theory' of anarchism without any consideration of 'the material, social, or psychological conditions under which anarchism might be a feasible mode of social organization'.[28] In other words, it identified anarchism with a commitment to individual decision-making (sometimes called private judgement) and divorced this commitment from the struggle to realize a particular socio-economic arrangement. Walter had a pithier view. Philosophical anarchism described a partial commitment to anarchy, the idea that 'society without government was attractive ... but not really possible ... anarchism in the head but not in the heart'.

What emerges from these treatments of anarchism? At first glance, the answer seems to be very little. In the matrix below some of the common typologies have been mapped onto the classical thinkers who have been identified by different writers with particular schools. Though there is some commonality in the table, what emerges from this matrix is a picture of confusion. The tendency of each new generation of writers is to have expanded the number of anarchist schools and to have redefined their membership, making the boundaries between schools increasingly diffuse.

Anarchist schools of thought: the classification of leading writers

	Seymour	De Cleyre	Kropotkin	Rocker	Walter
Individualism		Tucker	Stirner	Tucker, Proudhon	Godwin, Read, Stirner
Mutualism	Proudhon, Bakunin		Proudhon		Proudhon
Communism	Kropotkin		Kropotkin, Malatesta, Reclus	Godwin	Kropotkin, Goldman, Malatesta, Reclus, Rocker
Syndicalism			Pouget, Pelloutier	Rocker	Pouget, Pelloutier
Collectivism			Bakunin	Bakunin	Bakunin
Philosophic				Stirner	
Christian	Tolstoy		Tolstoy	Tolstoy	

Yet for all the confusion, the analysis of anarchist schools helps to shed some light on the nature of anarchism. The significance of the analysis lies in understanding the causes of the differences between the schools rather than their detailed delineation.

In his 1964 reader, *The Anarchists*, the American sociologist Irving Horowitz explained the fluidity of the boundaries between anarchist schools and their proliferation with reference to the different social, economic and political contexts in which anarchism operated. Anarchism had developed in response 'to changing social circumstances' and/or 'the internal tensions and strains of doctrine'.[29] Horowitz identified eight historic schools of thought: utilitarian, peasant, syndicalist, collectivist, conspiratorial, communist, individualist and pacifist anarchism to support his analysis. But he argued that his explanatory framework had an application that extended beyond this system of classification. These schools did not describe separate doctrines but alternative responses to particular historical, cultural and political conditions.

Horowitz's approach helps to explain why the same anarchist can be classified by others in completely different ways and it makes sense, for example, of the difference between Kropotkin's and Voltairine de Cleyre's conception of individualism. Kropotkin's immersion in Continental European philosophy suggested that anarchists like Voltairine de Cleyre were mutualists, not individualists. With her background in American radicalism and dissent, she classed herself as an individualist.

The emergence of new anarchist schools can also be explained by drawing on Horowitz's model. One of the striking features of much contemporary anarchism is the conviction that political and cultural conditions have altered so radically in the course of the twentieth century that the traditional schools of thought – those listed in the table – have become outmoded. As a result, as Horowitz suggests, anarchists who associate themselves with new schools believe that the struggles of the past must be jettisoned so that the challenges of the present can be confronted.

The main thrust of new anarchist thinking is the belief that the struggle by workers for economic emancipation no longer holds the key to anarchist revolution. The social ecology of Murray Bookchin, a major trend in new anarchism, is based on the belief that the transformation of west European societies in the late twentieth century no longer allows 'revolutionary consciousness [to] be developed ... around the issue of wage labor versus capital'.[30] The 'twenty-first century' anarchism discussed by Jon Purkis and James Bowen follows Bookchin's lead. Anarchism, they argue:

> ... is firmly rooted in the here and now ... The terrains of theory and action have changed, and now there are generations of activists operating in many fields of protest for whom the works of Kropotkin, Malatesta and Bakunin are as distant ... as the literary classics of ... Charles Dickens. The industrial age from which anarchism emerged operated on very different temporal and spatial levels from the present one, spawning political movements that addressed mostly issues of economic injustice and the instrumentalism of making sure that everyone had enough to eat. The dominant anarchist political vision of change was an insurrectionary one (the Revolution, on the barricades) ...
> Modern anarchism has long since needed a major overhaul ...[31]

Treading a similar path, John Zerzan, America's leading anarcho-primitivist, identifies the fundamental shift in anarchist thinking from 'traditional, production/progress-embracing outlook, toward

the primitivist critique or vision and its Luddite/feminist/decentral-ization/anti-civilization aspects'.[32] John Moore, who also situated himself in this school, argued that primitivism 'critiques the totality of civilisation from an anarchist perspective' and, in contrast to trad-itional leftists, primitivists did not 'worship the abstraction called "the proletariat"'.[33]

'New' anarchists are no more homogeneous in their response to these changes than their predecessors were in their treatment of class struggle. Indeed, new anarchists have little regard for each other and often profess a deep antipathy for each other's work (primitivists like Bob Black have been involved in very public disputes with Bookchin, as well as with 'old' style thinkers like Chomsky). Moreover, they point to a range of different sources of inspiration in developing their views. Writers like Bookchin have taken inspiration from the rise of the New Left and second wave feminism to explain the appar-ent redundancy of old anarchism. His social ecology has developed from a desire to probe the relationship posited by Marx between industrial development and political progress and from a concern to uncover the atomizing effects of the liberal market. Social ecology is about personal identity, the quality of the natural environment and building community in a way that allows individuals to live in har-mony with each other and with nature.

The inspiration for Purkis's and Bowen's anarchism celebrates philosophies which revel in the 'breakdown of absolute and mech-anistic interpretations of society', drawing anarchism to postmod-ernism, chaos theory, ecologism and feminist post-structuralism. Their anarchism is not as holistic as Bookchin's and is more strongly centred on the individual than the group. Moreover, it places a greater premium on the need to challenge prevailing habits and traditions of thought than it does on the necessity of remodelling the political environment. Indeed, in contrast to Bookchin who advo-cates the replacement of existing systems of political power with participatory, democratic forms ('municipal government'), Purkis and Bowen see anarchism as a perpetual process of struggle that brings individuals together in complex networks of action, facilitat-ing the expression of their differences rather than seeking finally to resolve them. This brand of anarchism, much influenced by the work of Michel Foucault, Giles Deleuze and Jean-François Lyotard, takes as one of its principal themes the avoidance of 'totalizing systems' – in both thought (the privileging of theories of knowledge; the search for theoretical certainty; the desire to design models for living) and in action (the imposition of rules or norms of behaviour; the formalization of patterns of organization).

Primitivists have found their inspiration in Stirner's individualism and the surrealist politics of the Situationalist International (SI) – a French neo-Marxist current of thought associated with Guy Debord and Raoul Vaneigem – that highlights the commodification, cultural repression and psychological manipulation ('spectacle') of individuals in capitalism. Their politics, like much new anarchism, is ecological. Yet their blending of ideas results in a brand of anarchism that disavows technology in favour of the 'feral': the condition of wildness, 'or existing in a state of nature, as freely occurring animals or plants; having reverted to the wild state from domestication'.[34] For many years, some women's groups have complained about the denaturalization of childbirth. Primitivism offers a similar critique of modern life, but extends it to the whole experience of life, to denounce 'civilization':

> Civilization is like a jetliner, noisy, burning up enormous amounts of fuel ...
>
> Civilization is like a 747, the filtered air, the muzak oozing over the earphones, a phony sense of security, the chemical food, the plastic trays, all the passengers sitting passively in the orderly row of padded seats staring at Death on the movie screen ...
>
> Civilization is like a 747, filled beyond capacity with coerced volunteers – some in love with the velocity, most wavering at the abyss of terror and nausea, yet still seduced by advertising and propaganda.[35]

Like postmoderns, primitivists reject systems of thought which purport to describe reality in terms of linear, progressive development. But rather than emphasizing theoretical diversity and rejecting the idea of certainty, primitivists argue that it is possible to grasp reality and to judge it. Moreover, where postmoderns look to multiple and endlessly shifting communities as a basis for anarchism, primitivists reject the possibility of realizing community in the body of the hegemon: technology.

Of course, many of the currents of thought now associated with new anarchism have been as inspirational to 'old' anarchist schools of thought. For example, Daniel Guérin combined an anarcho-syndicalist enthusiasm for workers' control with a deep admiration for Stirnerite individualism. Nonetheless, there has undoubtedly

Anarchism Old and New

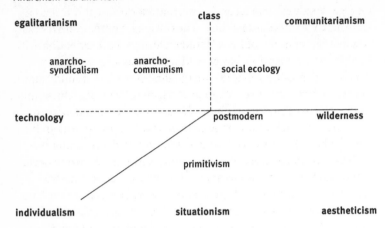

been a shift in anarchist thinking since the 1960s. The relationship of new to old anarchist schools is represented in the diagram above.

What light does Horowitz's framework shed on Eltzbacher's idea that anarchism can be defined by a unifying idea? The strength of Horowitz's approach is that it admits the possibility of such a definition whilst directing attention to the interpretative debates that have surrounded this idea. It supports Eltzbacher's claim that anarchist schools have something in common but it divorces this claim from the legalistic analysis which Eltzbacher applied and suggests, instead, that core values might be expressed in a variety of different ways, depending on the local historical, cultural and political contexts in which they are advanced. Moreover, it advances the examination of anarchism's positive content. As Murray Bookchin argues, anarchism is anti-statist but cannot be defined 'merely in terms of its *opposition* to the state' and should instead be regarded as a 'historical movement ... a social movement' operating 'in specific social contexts'.

As well as helping to delineate the spaces between anarchist schools, Horowitz's model also helps to define the parameters of anarchism in relation to other ideologies. The usefulness of his approach can be gauged by two recent boundary disputes. The first revolved around the possibility of accommodating radical Marxism (sometimes called left-libertarianism) within the anarchist fold and erupted in the late 1960s and '70s when disaffection with Soviet communism raised the profile of anarchist ideas within the New Left. The problem of libertarianism was identified by a range of anarchists, from communitarians like Murray Bookchin to individualists like George Woodcock and it acted as a catalyst for the establishment of the Anarchist International (AI). The complaint of these anarchists was that 'the children of Marx' (student leaders like Daniel Cohn-Bendit) were presenting 'basically Marxist ideas as anarchism'.[36] George Woodcock levelled the charge against Noam Chomsky and Daniel Guérin, accusing both men of selecting 'from anarchism those elements that may serve to diminish the contradictions in Marxist doctrines' and 'abandoning the elements that do not serve their purpose'. Their work enriched Marxism but impoverished anarchism.[37]

The second dispute came to prominence in the following decade and turned on the apparent openness of anarchism to 'anarcho-capitalism' or right-wing libertarianism. Anarcho-capitalism is no more a cohesive movement than any other school of anarchist thought. Its leading proponents, Murray Rothbard and Ayn Rand, had little regard for each other's work – indeed, Rothbard dismissed 'aynarchism' as an irrational and intolerant cult.[38] What unites anarcho-capitalists is the idea that the market is a natural form of organization in which individuals co-operate, productively, to their mutual benefit. From this starting point, Rothbard argued for the liberation of economic markets from political controls and Rand called for minimal government to protect and preserve capitalist markets. Unlike collectivist and communist schools of thought anarcho-capitalists suggest that the market is self-regulating and that the inequalities that result from exchange can be justified.

The boundary problem identified by left-leaning anarchists in the 1980s turned on the association between anarcho-capitalism and the doctrine 'rolling back the state' adopted by Ronald Reagan and Margaret Thatcher. 'Aynarchism' was most easily linked to this platform, not least because Randian libertarians worked with the Reagan administration – notably Alan Greenspan who was appointed in 1987 as chair of the US Federal Reserve. In contrast, Rothbard was highly critical of the administration and ridiculed the suggestion that the Reagan revolution to 'get government off our backs' expressed an anarcho-capitalist view.[39] But as John P. Clark notes, both versions of anarcho-capitalism had a historic root in anarchist thought, particularly in America: Benjamin Tucker, one of Eltzbacher's classical anarchists, had argued that '[a]narchism is consistent with Manchesterism' (or *laissez-faire* economics) and, at least in his early work, had defended the equal individual right to property. Indeed, Clark concluded, there were no clear boundaries between anarcho-capitalism and anarchist individualism.[40] A good number of anarchists find this conclusion unpalatable. José Pérez Adán argues the individualist case, representing what he calls reformist anarchism and anarcho-capitalism (particularly its Randian variant) as two distinct moral systems.[41] Peter Marshall takes a broader view but arrives at a similar conclusion. Anarcho-capitalists, he argues, prioritise self-interest and market rationality over voluntary co-operation and mutual support, alienating traditional anarchist individualists as well as anarcho-communists. He concludes, 'few anarchists would accept the "anarcho-capitalists" into the anarchists camp'.[42]

The blurring of the boundaries between anarchism and Marxism on the one hand, and liberalism on the other, has so disturbed some anarchists that they have attempted to define anarchism in a manner which marginalizes those schools deemed too close to the competing ideology. For example, in her dispute with George Woodcock, Marie Fleming argued that Woodcock emphasized the importance of anti-statism in anarchism precisely because he wanted to distinguish it from socialism. On the other side of the divide, anarcho-communists have sometimes defined anarchism as an anti-capitalist doctrine in order to divorce it from the perceived taint of individualism that anarchists like Woodcock believe to be foundational to the ideology. Horowitz's approach to anarchist schools suggests a different response: if anarchism is defined by an opposition to the state, as Eltzbacher suggests, anarchist anti-statism can be understood to refer to a spectrum of beliefs extending towards Chomsky and '68ers like Cohn-Bendit on one end of the spectrum and libertarians like Murray Rothbard on the other.

A number of important anarchist writers have endorsed such a view. For example, Rudolf Rocker found in anarchism 'the confluence of the two great currents which during and since the French Revolution have found such characteristic expression in the intellectual life of Europe: Socialism and Liberalism'. Nicolas Walter suggested that anarchists were like liberals in respect of freedom and like socialists in their demand for equality. Asked in 1995 whether he understood anarchism to be the 'equivalent of socialism with freedom', Chomsky echoes Rocker: anarchism draws from the 'best of Enlightenment and classical liberal thought'.[43] For each of these writers, the relationship of anarchism to liberalism and Marxism provides a useful route into the study of anarchist thought. History provides the most useful tool for analysing this relationship.

anarchist thought: history

In 1989 David Goodway bemoaned the poverty of anarchist histori-
ography, which he felt tended towards the uncritical hero-worship of
the classical anarchists and the failure of social historians to direct
their attention to the anarchist movement.[44] Little was known, he
argued, about this popular movement and what was known was
written by those who were hostile to it and/or who adopted theoretical approaches which were likely to shed only critical light on its
activities. Goodway's observations usefully highlight the polemical
nature of the historical debate about anarchism, the vehemence
with which Marxist historians, in particular, have attacked the anarchist movement and the consequent interest that non-Marxist historians have shown in the ideological division between anarchists and
Marxists. This division remains central to historians of anarchism.
For example, Nunzio Pernicone's recent work is based on the 'simple
premise' that 'Anarchism not Marxism, was the ideological current
that dominated and largely defined the Italian socialist movement
during its first fifteen years of development'.[45] Through such historical analyses it is possible both to illustrate the issues on which old-
style anarcho-communists (and others) split from other socialists
and to frame the changing relationship between anarchism and
liberalism.

The relationship between anarchists and Marxists has never been
happy. The historical antagonism is often personalized: after rebuff-
ing Marx's request in 1846 that the two co-operate, Proudhon
became the target for Marx's wrath. In 1847 he published *The
Poverty of Philosophy*, using all his intellectual powers to publicly
ridicule Proudhon's economic theory. In the 1860s, Bakunin took
the lead as Marx's anarchist opponent. He and Marx battled for
control of the First International (International Working Man's
Association, or IWMA), an organization that brought together
European radicals and socialists, falling out spectacularly in 1871.
As if to emphasize their personal enmity, Proudhon, Marx and
Bakunin happily heaped scorn on each other in the course of their
disputes. Yet the personalization of the debates between them is
misleading since it wrongly suggests a uniform and entirely hostile
anarchist critique of Marxism. Predictably, anarchists have assessed
Marxism in different ways and been willing to adopt some of Marx's
positions as their own. To give one example: in his review of

Proudhon's dispute with Marx, Bakunin argued that there was 'a good deal of truth in the merciless critique he [Marx] directed against Proudhon'.[46]

Relations between anarchists and Marxists remained fluid until 1921, when socialists decided whether or not to adhere to the Bolshevik International (Comintern). However in the nineteenth century socialists divided on a range of important issues about political organization and revolutionary strategy. These came to a head in the congresses of the Second International, which had been established on the centenary of the French Revolution in 1889. But it was possible to trace the roots of the argument to the dispute between Marx and Bakunin in the IWMA.

After 1871, when the First International effectively collapsed, socialists were split into two broad groups: 'centralists' and 'federalists' (or in later anarchist parlance 'authoritarians' and 'anti-authoritarians'). The followers of Marx were grouped in the first category and the followers of Bakunin in the second. The centralists supported in principle the formation of a workers' party, committed to involvement in the political process as a prelude to the seizure of power in revolution. They also argued for the tight control of IWMA's General Council to co-ordinate the revolutionary activity of the federated local sections. The federalists did not believe that socialist revolution could possibly succeed through political activity and were keen to maintain the autonomy of the IWMA's local sections. At a conference held in 1872 at St Imier, Switzerland, the federalists rejected totally the idea of revolutionary government as a means of securing socialist change, echoing the complaints that the *enragés* had made against the Jacobins.

The resolution marked a watershed in the development of European socialism, but it did not yet establish a clear distinction between anarchists and Marxists. The groups who split along federalist and centralist lines were themselves very diffuse: supporters of federalism included English trade unionists, for example. And not even those who had enjoyed the closest relations with Bakunin necessarily felt themselves bound by a distinctive programme. At the same time, as the followers of Marx in Europe began to organize in the 1870s and '80s working-class political parties, some activists within these organizations continued to adopt apparently 'anarchist' positions. Socialists turned out to be anarchists only when expelled from Marxist parties. Johann Most was one example, thrown out of the German Social Democratic Party (SPD) in 1880 when he refused to toe the party line on political action. It was not until after his expulsion that Most call himself an anarchist.

The anarchist-Marxist divide was solidified in the Second International when adherence to the policy of political action – which meant participation in parliamentary politics – was adopted as test of the International's membership. Those who were caught in this policy net represented a still diverse body of opinion. As Lenin noted, the '"practical" socialists of our day, have left *all* criticism of parliamentarism to the anarchists, and, on this wonderfully reasonable ground, they denounce all criticism of parliamentarism as "anarchism"!'[47] Yet the division was now supported by a good deal of theoretical embellishment and in countries like Japan, where socialist ideas took root later than in Europe, it became the central cleavage between anarchists and non-anarchists.[48] This was not surprising for in the course of the 1880s anarchists and Marxists had spent considerable time arguing about the parliamentary strategy and, in the process, both sides had developed coherent alternative understandings of the revolution and of the post-revolutionary society. By the 1890s the differences between the two sides were so visible that some Marxists felt able to argue that anarchism was not a form of socialism at all and that it described a competing ideology. The suggestion was contested fiercely by writers like Augustin Hamon. But in response to revolutionaries like Lenin, who argued that socialists agreed on the 'ends' of revolutionary struggle and disagreed only on the question of 'means', the anarchists also insisted that Marxist strategies revealed a faulty conception of the state.

Anarchist critiques of Marxist state theory had a number of dimensions. One set of arguments focused on the relationship between the state and capitalism. Bakunin's understanding was close to Marx's and he credited Marx with having demonstrated that the state's purpose was to uphold economic exploitation. Other leading theorists shared this view. Rudolf Rocker's version of the thesis was that as long 'as within society a possessing and a non-possessing group of human beings face one another in enmity ... the state will be indispensable to the possessing minority for the protection of its privileges'. Bakunin and Rocker also agreed that Marx had shown how the state's origins and development could be explained with reference to changes in the economic system. In Rocker's words, the modern state was 'just a consequence of capitalist economic monopoly, and the class divisions which this has set up in society, and merely serves the purpose of maintaining this status by every oppressive instrument of political power'. So where had Marx gone wrong? Bakunin's answer was that Marx's view of the state was too narrow and he had wrongly overplayed the role that economic forces had played in shaping the state to the detriment of others. As a result, Bakunin argued, he had overlooked the extent to which the state had developed as an independent force in history, separate from the system of economic exploitation that it functioned to uphold. Bakunin explained the difference between his position and Marx's in the following terms:

> [Marx] holds that the political condition of each country is always the product and the faithful expression of its economic situation ... He takes no account of other factors in history, such as the ever-present reaction of political, juridical, and religious institutions on the economic situation. He says: 'Poverty produces political slavery, the State.' But he does not allow this expression to be turned around, to say: 'Political slavery, the State, reproduces in its turn, and maintains poverty as a condition for its own existence; so that to destroy poverty, it is necessary to destroy the State!'[49]

Kropotkin had a slightly different understanding of the state's rise. Jean-Jacques Rousseau, the eighteenth-century philosopher, once claimed that government had been founded on the naïve willingness of the masses to accept the legitimacy of landowners' claims to the exclusive enjoyment of their property. Kropotkin's story was similar:

> The desire to dominate others and impose one's own will upon them ... the desire to surround oneself with comforts without producing anything ... these selfish, personal desires give rise to ... [a] current of habits and customs. The priest and the warrior, the charlatan who makes a profit out of superstition, and after freeing himself from the fear of the devil cultivates it in others; and the bully, who procures the invasion and pillage of his neighbors that he may return laden with booty and followed by slaves. These two, hand in hand, have succeeded in imposing upon primitive society customs advantageous to both of them, but tending to perpetuate the domination of the masses.[50]

But he agreed that the state existed to 'protect exploitation, speculation and private property' and characterized it as 'the by-product of the rapine of the people'. Kropotkin pinpointed Marx's error in his confusion of 'state' with 'government'.[51] Because he defined both as reflections of economic power, Marx was wrongly led to believe that it was possible to abolish the state simply by changing the form of government – by placing the control of government in socialist hands. Unlike Marxists, he argued, anarchists were not merely opponents of the transitory power of a particular regime or constitution. They opposed the decision-making apparatus or system of rule that all these regimes monopolized. His practical concern was that Marx had underestimated the threat of what Bakunin had called 'red bureaucracy': the potential for socialism to create a new form of oppression based on the control by workers' representatives of the state apparatus. Malatesta explained

> Social democrats start off from the principle that the State, government, is none other than the political organ of the dominant class. In a capitalistic society, they say, the State necessarily serves the interests of the capitalists and ensures for them the right to exploit the workers; but that in a socialist society, when private property were to be abolished, and ... class distinctions would disappear, then the State would represent everybody and become the impartial organ representing the social interests of all members of society. [52]

A second set of criticisms examined the state role as an instrument of revolutionary change. These critiques had two variations: one focused on the idea of dictatorship and the other on the theoretical assumptions that underpinned the parliamentary strategy. The first line of attack followed as a corollary to the Bakuninist critique of bureaucracy. Anarchist critics noted that the dictatorship of the proletariat, endorsed by Marx as a necessary means of securing the victory of the workers, was supposed to be both temporary and non-dictatorial. Yet by placing workers' representatives in a position where they could use violence against designated class enemies, critics argued that it would inevitably become a permanent form of oppression. As Rocker argued:

> Dictatorship is a definite form of state power ... it is the proclamation of the wardship of the toiling people, a guardianship forced upon the masses by a tiny minority. *Even if its supporters are animated by the very best intentions*, the iron logic of facts will always drive them into the camp of extremest [sic] despotism ... the pretence that the so-called *dictatorship of the proletariat* is something different ... is only a sophisticated trick to fool simpletons. Such a thing as the dictatorship of a class is utterly unthinkable, since there

will always be involved merely the dictatorship of a particular party which takes it upon itself to speak *in the name of a class* ...[53]

Turning to the second variation, critics like Gustav Landauer and Kropotkin's friend, Varlaam Cherkezov, argued that the parliamentary strategy was posited on an idea of historical development that was overly mechanistic. Marx, Landauer argued, had wrongly believed that he had discovered a law of economic development from which the inevitable collapse of capitalism and victory of socialism could be deduced. Faith in his law had misled Marxists to believe that they could play a waiting game in state legislatures, building up their political strength until such time that the moment of crisis arrived and they could use their party machines to socialize the economic system. As Cherkezov put it, Marxists believed that it 'is enough that the workers should vote for members of parliament who call themselves Socialists, that the number of these MPs should increase to the extent of a majority in the House, that they should decree State Collectivism or Communism'. The idea was ludicrous for it supposed that 'all exploiters will peaceably submit to the decision of parliament' and that 'capitalists will have no choice but unresisting submission'.[54]

A final set of criticisms focused on the class bias of Marx's state theory. Here, the focus of the anarchist critique was Marx's preoccupation with proletarian liberation and his disregard of rural workers and the underclass – the unemployed, the outcast and the dispossessed – as subjects for liberation. Bakunin's worry was that Marx's scientific theory was exclusively focused on the liberation of the urban working class and that the communist revolution would lead to the oppression of all other workers in the name of economic progress. Landauer shared Bakunin's fear and against Marx's view argued: '*The struggle for socialism is a struggle for the land; the social question is an agrarian question*'.[55]

Many anarchists believe that these nineteenth-century debates were finally played out in the Russian Revolution. In his eyewitness account of events, Voline remembered how in 1917 the Bolsheviks launched 'slogans which until then had particularly and insistently been voiced by the Anarchists: *Long live the Social Revolution!*' For the anarchists this call described '*a really social act*: a transformation which would take place outside of all political and statist organizations ...'. It meant '*destruction of the State and capitalism at the same time*, and the birth of a new society based on another form of social organization'. For the Bolsheviks, however, the slogan meant 'resurrection of the State after the abolition of the bourgeois State – that is to say, the creation of a powerful new State for the purpose of "constructing Socialism"'.[56] Whilst many modern anarchists – from anarcho-syndicalists to postmodernists – classify themselves as anti-capitalists rather than anti-statists, the experience of the revolution and the subsequent creation of the Soviet State have added weight to the view that anarchism revolves around the rejection of the state, since this is the point on which anarchism and Marxism divide. In 1922 in a bad-tempered exchange with the 'left Bolshevik' Nikolai Bukharin, Luigi Fabbri argued:

> The state is more than an outcome of class division; it is ... the creator of privilege ... Marx was in error in thinking that once classes had been abolished the state would die a natural death ... The state will not die away unless it is deliberately destroyed, just as capitalism will not cease to exist unless it is put to death through expropriation.
> ... And, let us say it again, the anarchists have pointed this out – in their polemics with social democrats – times without number from 1880 up to the present day.[57]

One of the effects of the formal division of socialists into anarchist and Marxist camps has been to encourage anarchists to re-evaluate their relationship to liberalism. Bruised by their knowledge of the tyranny of Soviet socialism, twentieth-century anarchists in particular reasserted their commitment to the philosophy of liberalism and offered robust defences of the civic freedoms with which liberals are traditionally associated.

The theoretical alignment of anarchism with liberalism has a historical root. William Godwin's anarchism was firmly grounded in a tradition of radicalism informed by scientific reason. Bakunin, too, celebrated the idea of reason and identified in liberalism a principle of rationality and of scientific thought that he linked with emancipation and progress. Though he complained that the benefits of scientific knowledge extended to 'only ... a very small portion of society', he believed that liberal science would provide the foundation for integral or all-round education in anarchy. Developing this idea, the Spanish anarchist Francisco Ferrer commented:

> Those imaginary products of the mind, *a priori* ideas, and all the absurd and fantastical fictions hitherto regarded as truth and imposed as directive principles on human conduct, have for some

time past incurred the condemnation of reason and the resentment of conscience ... Science is no longer the patrimony of a small group of privileged individuals; its beneficent rays more or less consciously penetrate every rank of society. On all sides traditional errors are being dispelled by it; by the confident procedure of experience and observation it enables us to attain accurate knowledge and criteria in regard to natural objects and the laws which govern them. With indisputable authority it bids men lay aside for ever their exclusivisms and privileges, and it offers itself as the controlling principle of human life, seeking to imbue all with a common sentiment of humanity.[58]

The relationship between anarchism and rational science blossomed in the 1880s and '90s, largely under the influence of Kropotkin and Reclus who extended Bakunin's ideas to develop an empirically based theory of anarchism. In their various geographical and sociological writings they developed Bakunin's argument, that prevailing methods of scientific investigation held the key to social well-being, in an attempt to demonstrate the naturalness of anarchy. Anarchists like Malatesta complained that Kropotkin confused science with morals and that his anarchism was too mechanistic. But the idea that anarchism had a foundation in empirical science was difficult to resist. Indeed, the claim that Marx had founded 'scientific' socialism provided an additional spur for anarchists to appropriate liberal science and harness it to their own cause because it provided a means to undermine and ridicule this claim.

Notwithstanding Malatesta's reservations the scientific model dominated twentieth-century anarchism. In a discussion of Alex Comfort's work, David Goodway comments:

Historically ... anarchists have ... regarded science as a force for progress: being the revelation of the structure of the natural world ... and hence in opposition to the mystifying claims of religious superstition, of class rule and, after 1917, of ideology. It has only been in the late twentieth century that science and radical politics have become uncoupled ...[59]

Anarchists continue to work within this paradigm. The Anarchist International represents itself as a 'non-sectarian' and 'non-dogmatic' organization, open to 'all libertarian tendencies'. But it is also 'non-dialectical and non-metaphysical', committed to 'the method of modern science, introduced by Kropotkin ... in short the anarchist scientifical way of thinking' (Bulletin of the Anarchist International). In his well-known pamphlet *Listen, Anarchist!* Chaz Bufe also defends science, rationality and technology as the only permissible tools of anarchist dissent. In rather different ways, Rothbard and Rand also ground anarchism in an idea of reason. Rothbard's work is based on a conception of natural law and Rand's on what she calls 'objective' law, similarly discoverable through the exercise of reason.[60] The 'post-objectivist' George H. Smith captures the gist of the idea. Anarchism, he argues,

> is grounded in the belief that we are fully capable, through reason, of discerning the principles of justice; and that we are capable, through rational persuasion and voluntary agreement, of establishing whatever institutions are necessary for the preservation and enforcement of justice.[61]

The theoretical alignment of anarchism with liberal science was paralleled by a reassessment of liberalism's political value. Some anarchist schools had long seen a positive element in liberal thought and like liberals claimed liberty as one of their primary goals. Yet not all groups of anarchists have asserted the priority of liberty with equal force. So-called individualists – particularly in America – have tended to be the most vocal advocates of liberty, identifying anarchism firmly with the defence of rights. Indeed, some writers have argued that liberal anarchism is a peculiarly American phenomenon. In her analysis of the relationship of anarchism to American political culture Voltairine de Cleyre argued that independence of thought, freedom from the tyranny of arbitrary government and the guarantee of civic rights were the hallmarks of both anarchist and liberal traditions. The patriots of the Revolution 'took their starting point for deriving a minimum government upon the same sociological ground that the modern Anarchist derives the no-government theory; viz., that equal liberty is the political ideal'.[62] Ayn Rand also argued that American anarchism had been shaped by the revolutionary tradition. Europeans, she added, had never 'fully grasped' the American philosophy of the Rights of Man and remained firmly wedded to the competing principle of the common good. The Scottish anti-parliamentarian, Guy Aldred, offered a less culturally determined account, extending the American tradition back to the English homeland. The 'English-speaking race, on both sides of the Atlantic, have by persecution at the stake, by jail, and exile, made the English tongue the tongue of liberty and of freedom'.[63]

Traditionally, European anarcho-communists have been rather more cynical about the value of liberal rights in the absence of economic equality. Proudhon defined liberty in terms of the necessity to maintain 'equality in the means of production and equivalence in exchanges'.[64] Similarly, whilst Bakunin famously declared himself a 'fanatical lover of liberty', he also argued that workers told about political freedom would rightly reply, '*Do not speak of freedom: poverty is slavery*'.[65] In the 1870s Kropotkin contrasted the formal rights guaranteed by liberal states with the effective rights yet to be claimed by the oppressed. The first were tools of oppression and the second powers to be extracted from the state. There was a clear gulf between the two.

The rise to power of the Bolsheviks in the Russian Revolution was not the only event that led anarchists to re-evaluate the significance of liberal rights. The emergence of fascism has also helped to reinforce anarchist commitments to liberal freedoms and strengthened the belief that these freedoms can only be realized in a non-exploitative stateless society. Indeed, many European anarchist groups – particularly in France, Spain and Italy – continue to identify their struggle for freedom with a commitment against fascism. Nevertheless the Russian Revolution certainly helped to concentrate anarchist minds on the independent value of these freedoms. As Voline argued:

> A *true* revolution can only take its flight, evolve, attain its objectives, if it has an environment of the free circulation of revolutionary ideas concerning the course to follow, and the problems to be solved. This liberty is as indispensable to the Revolution as air is to respiration. That is why ... the dictatorship which leads inevitably to the suppression of *all* freedom of speech, press, organization, and action – even for the revolutionary tendencies, except for the party in power – is *fatal* to true revolution.[66]

Reviewing, in 1926, the old distinctions between individualists and communists, Malatesta still maintained that the former attached too much importance to 'an abstract concept of freedom' but nevertheless arrived at a unified conception of anarchism as 'all and only those forms of life that respect liberty'.[67]

Anarchists have continued to develop this interest in political liberty in the post-war period. British anarchists in the Freedom group paid particular attention to the issue of censorship, particularly on the grounds of indecency. Writers for the journal *Anarchy* opposed with equal conviction calls to ban works from Mara Bryant's recording, *Please, Mister, Don't You Touch My Tomato*, to D.H. Lawrence's *Lady Chatterley's Lover* on the grounds that they supported freedom of speech and expression. In a similar vein, one of the declared objectives of the French Fédération Anarchiste is 'the absolute right for all individuals to express their opinions'.[68] Recently one anti-globalizer has offered the memorable definition of anarchism as 'liberalism on steroids'.

The relationship between anarchism, Marxism and liberalism helps to contextualize two recent anarchist debates. The first revolves around the relative importance of individual expression and creative experimentation, and/or the desirability of bringing individuals together in community over the need to engage in class struggle to liberate peoples from exploitation. New anarchists typically emphasize the importance of the first two whilst 'old' anarchists give greater weight to the last. The second debate reflects a recent shift amongst primitivists and postmoderns against liberal rationalism and science. For primitivists, liberal rationality expresses a faulty approach towards reality: one that asserts the superiority of the intellect over sense and feeling. For postmoderns it represents a mistaken idea of truth and reality: neither intellect nor feeling can capture either, there are only diverse and multiple interpretations. Yet both groups are hostile to the scientific, rationalist tradition that has dominated anarchist thought. Lawrence Jarach's primitivist critique of Chaz Bufe's 'ultra-rationalist and moralist perspective' and his 'liberal leftist' commitment to ' "civil liberties" ' is one example of the recent trend.[69] 'Joff's' poststructuralist/postmodern critique of Bookchin's developmental, naturalistic science is another.[70]

In addition, the history of the relationship between anarchism and liberalism places anarchism on a broader spectrum of ideas than the bi-partite division of Marxism and anarchism allows, fleshing out anarchism's ideological content. Drawing on this history Stuart Christie and Albert Meltzer situated anarchism in a framework that distinguished between 'individualistic' and 'totalitarian' ways of life, and 'capitalistic' and 'socialistic' forms of work.[71]

Mapping Anarchy

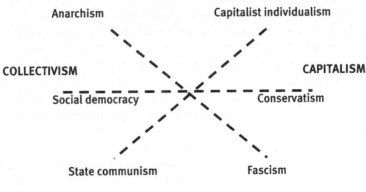

INDIVIDUALISM

Anarchism   Capitalist individualism

COLLECTIVISM   CAPITALISM

Social democracy   Conservatism

State communism   Fascism

TOTALITARIANISM

summary

This chapter has examined three different approaches to the analysis of anarchist ideas, the first focusing on core concepts abstracted from the writings of 'classical' anarchists, the second based on the division of anarchists into schools and the third examining the history of anarchist ideas. Through these analyses I have argued that anarchism should be considered as an ideology defined by the rejection of the state. This core idea should not be treated in abstract, but as a principle, first articulated in the course of a particular historical debate between socialists, that can be filled in a variety of different ways. The next chapter considers in more detail some of the ways in which anarchists have conceptualized their rejection of the state and the ideas of freedom that they have drawn from their critiques.

further reading

Paul Avrich, *Anarchist Portraits* (Princeton, NJ: Princeton University Press, 1988)

Daniel Guérin, *Anarchism* (New York: Monthly Review Press, 1970)

Daniel Guérin, *No Gods, No Masters*, 2 vols. (London: AK Press, 1998)

James Joll, *The Anarchists*, 2nd edn. (London: Methuen, 1979)
Peter Marshall, *Demanding the Impossible* (London: HarperCollins,
   1992)
David Miller, *Anarchism* (London: J.M. Dent & Sons, 1984)
Max Nettlau, *A Short History of the Anarchist Movement* (London:
   Freedom Press, 1996)
Paul Thomas, *Karl Marx and the Anarchists* (London: Routledge &
   Kegan Paul, 1980)
Nicolas Walter, *About Anarchism* (London: Freedom Press, 2002)
George Woodcock, *Anarchism* (Penguin: Harmondsworth, 1979)

The following anarchist texts (and more) can be accessed at
   http://dwardmac.pitzer.edu/Anarchist_Archives
Noam Chomsky, *Notes on Anarchism*
Emma Goldman, *Anarchism: What it Really Stands For*
Peter Kropotkin, *Anarchism*
Errico Malatesta, *Anarchy*
Elisée Reclus, *Anarchy by an Anarchist*

links

Anarchy: A Journal of Desire Armed: http://www.anarchymag.org
Egoist Archive: http://www.nonserviam.com/egoistarchive/index.html
Online anarchy: http://www.infoshop.org
Primitivism: http://www.primitivism.com/primitivism.htm
Ayn Rand Institute: http://www.aynrand.org/site/PageServer
Murray Rothbard Archive: http://www.lewrockwell.com/rothbard/
   rothbard-arch.html
Kate Sharpley Library (anarchist history and research):
   http://www.katesharpleylibrary.net
Situationist International: http://www.nothingness.org/SI
Spunk Press (anarchist resources): http://www.spunk.org
Social anarchism: http://www.socialanarchism.org

notes

1. G.D.H. Cole in Horowitz, *The Anarchists* (New York: Dell Publishing,
   1964).
2. G. Woodcock, *Anarchism* (Harmondsworth: Penguin, 1979), 8–9.

3.　*Dictionnaire de L'Académie Française* at http://colet.uhicago.edu/cgi-bin

4.　P.-J. Proudhon, *What is Property?* (London: William Reeves, 1969), 259–60.

5.　M. Bakunin, *On Anarchism*, ed. S. Dologff (Montreal: Black Rose, 1980), 57.

6.　P. Kropotkin, *Words of a Rebel*, ed. G. Woodcock (Montreal: Black Rose, 1992), 79–80.

7.　A. Berkman, *ABC of Anarchism* (London: Freedom Press, 1980), 1–2.

8.　Anarchist Media Group, *Everything You Ever Wanted to Know About Anarchism But Were Afraid to Ask* (Cardiff: Black Sheep/Dark Star/Rebel Press, 1988), 3.

9.　D. Rooum, *What is Anarchism?* (London: Freedom Press, 1993), 3.

10.　P. Kropotkin quoted by J.J. Martin, introduction to P. Eltzbacher, *Anarchism: Exponents of the Anarchist Philosophy* (London: Freedom Press, 1960), vii.

11.　R.B. Fowler, 'The Anarchist Tradition of Political Thought', *Western Political Quarterly* (1972), 25: 738.

12.　G. Crowder, 'Anarchism', *Anarchist Studies* (1996) 2 (4):156.

13.　D. Guérin, *No Gods, No Masters*, vol. 1 (London: AK Press, 1998), 3.

14.　D. Guérin, *Anarchism* (New York & London: Monthly Review Press, 1970), 6.

15.　N. Walter, *About Anarchism* (London: Freedom Press, 2002), 27–8.

16.　A. Carlson, *Anarchism in Germany* (Metuchen N.J.: Scarecrow Press, 1972), 1–4.

17.　K. Widmer, 'Arguing Anarchism', *Social Anarchism* (2000), 27 at http://library.nothingness.org/articles/SA/en/display/337

18.　P. Eltzbacher, *Anarchism: Exponents of the Anarchist Philosophy* (London: Freedom Press, 1960), 189.

19.　M. Fleming, *The Geography of Freedom* (Montreal: Black Rose, 1988), 23–4.

20.　G. Esenwein, *Anarchist Ideology and the Working Class Movement in Spain, 1868–1898* (Oxford: University of California Press), 147; M. Nettlau, *A Short History of Anarchism* (London: Freedom Press, 1996), 195–203.

21.　V. de Cleyre, 'The Making of an Anarchist', *Quiet Rumours* (London: Dark Star, n.d.), 51–3.

22.　J. Moore, 'Maximalist Anarchism/Anarchist Maximalism', *Social Anarchism* (1998), 25 at http://library.nothingness.org/articles/SA/en/display/134

23.　R. Boston, 'Conversations About Anarchism', in C. Ward (ed.), *A Decade of Anarchy* (London: Freedom Press, 1987), 11.

24. H. Seymour, *The Two Anarchisms* (London, 1894).

25. de Cleyre, 'The Making of An Anarchist', 51.

26. P. Kropotkin, 'Anarchism' in R. Baldwin (ed.) *Kropotkin's Revolutionary Pamphlets* (New York: Dover, 1970), 293–6.

27. R. Rocker, *Anarcho-Syndicalism* (London: Phoenix Press, n.d.), 16.

28. R.P. Wolff, *In Defense of Anarchism* (New York: Harper & Row, 1970), viii.

29. I. Horowitz, *The Anarchists* (New York: Dell Publishing, 1964), 30–55.

30. M. Bookchin, 'Anarchism: Past and Present', in H. Ehrlich (ed.) *Reinventing Anarchism Again* (Edinburgh: AK Press, 1996), 24.

31. J. Purkis and J. Bowen, *Twenty-First Century Anarchism* (London: Cassell, 1997), 3.

32. J. Zerzan, *Running on Emptiness: The Pathology of Civilization* (Los Angeles: Feral House, 2002), 195.

33. J. Fliss, *Interview with John Moore*, http://www.insurgentdesire.org.uk/ jminterview.htm

34. J. Zerzan, *Future Primitive and Other Essays* (New York: Autonomedia, 1994), 144.

35. T. Fulano, 'Civilization is like a jetliner', in J. Zerzan and A. Carnes (eds), *Questioning Technology: Tool, Toy or Tyrant?* (Philadelphia: New Society Publishers, 1991), 69.

36. The Anarchist International, *Bulletin of the Anarchist International*, http://www.wassamattayou.com/anarchy/ai.html

37. G. Woodcock, 'Chomsky's Anarchism' in *Anarchism and Anarchists* (Kingston, Ontario: Quarry Press, 1992), 228.

38. M. Rothbard, *The Sociology of the Ayn Rand Cult* (1972), http://lewrockwell.com/rothbard/rothbard23.html

39. M. Rothbard, *Ronald Reagan: An Autopsy*, http://www.lewrockwell.com/ rothbard/rothbard60.html

40. J. Clark, *The Anarchist Moment* (Montreal: Black Rose, 1986), 132.

41. J. Pérez Adán, *Reformist Anarchism* (Braunton, Devon: Merlin Books, 1992), 175–98.

42. P. Marshall, *Demanding the Impossible* (London: HarperCollins, 1992), 565.

43. N. Chomsky, *Anarchism, Marxism and Hope for the Future* (Montreal: Kersplebedeb, 1995), 3.

44. D. Goodway, *For Anarchism: History, Theory and Practice* (London: Routledge, 1989), 6.

45. N. Pernicone, *Italian Anarchism* (New Jersey: Princeton University Press, 1993), 3.

46. M. Bakunin, *Statism and Anarchy* (Cambridge: Cambridge University Press, 1990), 142.

47. V.I. Lenin, *The State and Revolution* (Moscow: Progress Publishers, 1977), 45.

48. C. Tsuzuki, 'Anarchism in Japan' in D. Apter and J. Joll (eds), *Anarchism Today* (London: Macmillan, 1971), 106.

49. Bakunin, 'Letter to La Liberté' in *On Anarchism*, ed. Sam Dolgoff (Montreal: Black Rose, 1980), 281–2.

50. Kropotkin, *Revolutionary Pamphlets*, 203.

51. Kropotkin, *The State: Its Historic Role* (London: Freedom Press, 1943), 10.

52. E. Malatesta, *Life and Ideas*, ed. V. Richards (London: Freedom Press, 1977), 143–4.

53. Rocker, *Anarcho-syndicalism*, 44.

54. V. Cherkezov, *Pages of Socialist History* (New York: C.B. Cooper, 1902), 26.

55. G. Landauer, *For Socialism* (St Louis, Missouri: Telos Press, 1978), 134.

56. Voline, *The Unknown Revolution* (Montreal: Black Rose, 1975), 210–11.

57. L. Fabbri, 'Anarchy and "Scientific" Communism', *The Poverty of Statism* (Orkney: Cienfuegos Press), 20–1.

58. F. Ferrer, *The Origin and Ideals of the Modern School* (London: Watts & Co., 1913), 19.

59. D. Goodway, introduction to *Alex Comfort: Writings Against Power and Death* (London: Freedom Press, 1994), 17.

60. A. Rand, 'What is Capitalism?' in *Capitalism: The Unknown Ideal* (New York: Signet, 1967), 22–3; M. Rothbard, *The Ethics of Liberty* (New York: New York University Press, 2002), 12–15.

61. G.H. Smith, *In Defence of Rational Anarchism*, 1997, http://folk.uio.no/thomas/po/rational-anarchism.html

62. V. de Cleyre, *Anarchism and American Traditions* (San Francisco: Sharp Press, 1989), 6.

63. G. Aldred, *A Call to Manhood* (Glasgow: Strickland Press, 1944), 16.

64. Proudhon, *What is Property?*, 272.

65. M. Bakunin, in R. Cutler (ed.), *The Basic Bakunin* (New York: Prometheus Books, 1992), 107.

66. Voline, *Unknown Revolution*, 188.

67. E. Malatesta, 'Communism and Individualism' in V. Richards (ed), *The Anarchist Revolution* (London: Freedom Press, 1995), 14–16.

68. http://www.federation-anarchiste.org/documents/princilesgb.html

69. L. Jarach, *A Few Comments on Bufe*, http://pub5ezboard.com/
ftheanarchyboardanarchy.shoMessage?topicID+112.topic
70. 'Joff', *Anti-Humanist Anarchism*, http://library.nothingness.org/
articles/anar/en/display/306
71. S. Christie and A. Meltzer, *The Floodgates of Anarchy* (London:
Kahn & Averill, 1984), 103–5.

anarchist rejections of the state

Anarchism ... is more than anti-statism. But government (the state) because it claims ultimate sovereignty and the right to outlaw or legitimate particular sovereignties, and because it serves the interests, predominantly, of those who possess particular spheres of power, stands at the centre of the web of social domination; it is appropriately, the central focus of anarchist critique.

(David Wieck, in *Reinventing Anarchy*, p. 139)

... the modern State is the organizational form of an authority founded upon arbitrariness and violence ... It relies upon oppressive centralism, arising out of the direct violence of a minority deployed against the majority. In order to enforce and impose the legality of its system, the State resorts not only to the gun and money, but also to potent weapons of psychological pressure. With the aide [sic] of such weapons, a tiny group of politicians enforces psychological repression of an entire society, and, in particular, of the toiling masses, conditioning them in such a way as to divert their attention from the slavery instituted by the State.

(Nestor Makhno, *The Struggle Against the State and Other Essays*, p. 56)

The state has generated some of the most powerful images in anarchist writing. Following the German philosopher Friedrich Nietzsche, Emma Goldman described the state as a 'cold monster', an inhuman and murderous being. Fredy Perlman, a writer associated with primitivism, used the image of Leviathan referring to the idea of the state as outlined by the seventeenth-century British philosopher Thomas Hobbes to describe it as 'a monstrous body ... without any life of its own ... a dead thing, a huge cadaver'. In whichever way they choose to describe it the distinctive claim that anarchists make about the state is that it is undesirable and unnecessary.

Anarchists have analysed the state in a number of ways. Some have looked at the state's formation. Kropotkin's is probably the best-known historical account of the state's development but in recent years John Zerzan and Fredy Perlman have also returned to its history. Others have looked at the state's functions, typically identifying the state with exploitation or monopoly. A significant number have attempted to describe the state by looking at the abstract concepts with which it has been associated in the history of ideas.

This chapter reviews some of these analyses, first looking at the ways anarchists have defined abstract ideas of government, authority and power. There are a number of reasons for starting here. First, the analysis of these ideas has occupied a central place in anarchist theorizing – indeed, anarchists have often defined anarchy in terms of their abolition. Second, because anarchists have defined and combined these ideas in a variety of ways, their analysis helps to capture the scope of the anarchist critiques. Third, anarchist critiques of government, authority and power help to establish the limits of the anarchists' rejection of the state, pinpointing the difference between illegitimate and legitimate rule. Finally, anarchist critiques of these ideas provide a context for the discussions of liberty. Some theorists – and many anarchists – have argued that the commitment to liberty defines anarchist thought. However, in contrast to liberal thought, to which anarchism is indebted, anarchists do not believe that liberty requires law. To the contrary, anarchist conceptions of freedom are posited on the state's abolition.

government, authority, power and the state

Critics of anarchism have sometimes suggested that anarchists use concepts of government, authority and power as synonyms for the state rather than tools of analysis. When they call for the abolition of the state, critics argue, they also mean to reject government, authority and power. This critique of the anarchist position is not entirely groundless since anarchists have often rejected these concepts in blanket terms, habitually defining anarchy in terms of their abolition. Anarchy, Malatesta argued, 'comes from Greek and its literal meaning is WITHOUT GOVERNMENT: the condition of a people who live without a constituted authority, without government'.[1] Sébastien Faure substituted authority for government. An anarchist, he argued, is someone who 'denies Authority and fights against'.[2] Likewise John Zerzan defines anarchism as a synonym for anti-authoritarianism. For George Woodock, anarchism was about giving 'men ... the bread of brotherly love, and not the stones of power – of any power'.[3] John Moore also identified anarchism with the rejection of power. In a careful analysis of anarchist poststructuralism, he rejected the possibility of distinguishing between 'suppressive' and 'productive' forms of power, insisting that 'no relationships of power are acceptable'.[4]

What do anarchists mean by these claims? What are their specific concerns? By government, anarchists tend to think of a particular system of rule, based on violence. In authority they consider the social relationships sustained by this system, and in power they consider the means by which government secures its authority. Each concept is considered in turn.

government and the state

Many anarchists argue that the characteristic feature of government in the state is violence. The raw view of this relationship is that governments, be they 'absolute or constitutional, monarchy or republic, Fascist, Nazi or Bolshevik', rule by the use of physical force. The qualified view is that governments prefer not to rely on the open use of force and that the ability of governors to secure popular consent usually makes physical coercion unnecessary.[5] Some anarchists define the state in terms very similar to those offered by the German sociologist, Max Weber. For example, Rothbard argues that the 'state is that organization in society which attempts to maintain a monopoly of the use of force and violence in a given territorial area'.[6] Moreover, like Weber, anarchists tend to explain the actual incidence of government violence in Machiavellian terms. As a writer in *Freedom* put it, '[e]very government governs by a combination of deceit and coercion. The crude ones more by coercion, the clever ones more by deceit'. In constitutional and democratic regimes, where governments feel secure, they 'allow a greater degree of latitude to their subjects' and govern through fraud. Where they lack popular support and 'are too afraid to allow any measure of liberty at all', deceit fails and government relies on violence to force the people into submission.[7] Anarchists point to the behaviour of governments in moments of tension or crisis to support this thesis. For example, British anarchists argue that the 1984–5 miners' strike provided graphic illustration of the government's willingness to crush dissent by force. More recently, activists have pointed to police actions at anti-globalization rallies to make the case. Protests at the Genoa G8 summit in July 2001 made headlines after the killing of Carlo Giuliani, a young protestor, and the beating of journalists and protestors in a night-raid led by the Italian *Carabinieri*. One anarchist gives this account of events:

> The police entered: the media and the politicians were kept out. And they beat people. They beat people who had been sleeping, who held up their hands in a gesture of innocence and cried out, 'Pacifisti! Pacifisti!'
>
> They beat the men and the women. They broke bones, smashed teeth, shattered skulls. They left blood on the walls, on the windows, a pool of it in every spot where people had been sleeping. When they have finished their work, they brought in the ambulances …
>
> This really happened. Not back in the nineteen thirties, but on the night of July 21 and the morning of July 22, 2001. Not in some third world country, but in Italy: prosperous, civilized, sunny Italy.

The conclusion drawn by this activist is

> That the police could carry out such a brutal act openly … means that they do not expect to be held accountable for their actions. Which means that they had support from higher up, from more powerful politicians …[8]

Noting that a number of leading anarchists – Bakunin, Kropotkin and Tolstoy – were Russians, the American political scientist Paul Douglas argued that anarchism was a response to autocracy and that its 'surest cure' was 'for the states to lead the good life'.[9] Yet the surprising conclusion drawn by some anarchists is that the latent violence of constitutional government is worse than the overt violence of dictatorial rule. In the constitutional state citizens enter into a sort of Faustian pact, consenting to violence in return for civil rights and welfare benefits. John Zerzan has recently put this case. As taxpayers to government 'we're all implicated' in the violence committed in our name. Giving the lie to Douglas, Tolstoy offered a similar view, contrasting the position of subjects and citizens:

> A subject of the most despotic Government can be completely free although he may be subjected to cruel violence on the part of the

authorities he has not established; but a member of a constitutional State is always a slave because, imagining that he has participated or can participate in his Government, he recognizes the legality of all violence perpetrated upon him ...[10]

Government violence is not restricted to the internal sphere – it has an external aspect. As Emma Goldman argued, government is 'an instrument of competitive struggle' which strives constantly to expand its influence and prestige. For Rothbard:

> The natural tendency of the State is to expand its powers and exter-
> nally such expansion takes place by conquest of a territorial area.
> Unless a territory is stateless or uninhabited, any such expansion
> involves inherent conflict of interest between one set of State rules
> and another.[11]

Governments pursue the state's external interests in the same way as they secure its domestic dominance: by a combination of force and fraud. For example, in recent criticism of US policy Noam Chomsky links what he calls government-sponsored terrorism to aid and arms programmes. In the 1980s he argues, US administrations turned Central America and the Middle East 'into a graveyard'. Chomsky continues: '[h]undreds of thousands of people were massacred – two hundred thousand, approximately' creating over a million refugees and orphans and subjecting 'great masses' of others to torture and 'every conceivable form of barbarism'. In addition, the US uses trade sanctions, 'in order to crush peoples' lives'. Long-standing embargos have prevented food and medicines reaching Cuba, dramatically lowering health and nutrition rates amongst Cubans and causing a 'significant rise in suffering and death'.[12]

Anarchists have offered psychological and material explanations for the violence of government. The nineteenth-century writer Charlotte Wilson argued that government was an expression of a 'tendency towards domination', a natural though destructive instinct present in all individuals.[13] The psychological explanation has a number of variations. In Rand's hands, it is tied to a tribal, primor-dial urge (born in Europe) to conquer, loot, enslave and annihilate. Anarcha-feminists offer a contrasting view, re-examining the issue of violence through the prism of feminist critique. On these accounts, Wilson's observed tendency becomes gender-specific. Flick Ruby argues that government violence turns on men's willingness and ability to dominate women. In her reflections on the role of women in anti-war campaigns she comments: '[i]f the peace movement is to be successful in putting an end to war, it must work to eliminate the sex role system which is killing us all by rewarding dominating aggressive behaviour in men'.[14] The Guerrilla Girls explore a similar theme, imagining an estrogen-bombed world where troops in conflict zones 'throw down their guns, hug each other, say it was "all their fault", and clean up the mess'.[15] Perlman, too, understands government as an expression of maleness. With the rise of Leviathan, he argues, 'women become debased, domesticated, abused and instrumentalized, and then scribes proceed to erase the memory that women were ever important'.[16]

Since the 1960s anarchists have increasingly added an ecological dimension to the argument. Murray Bookchin associates the emergence of government-systems with the historic re-casting of the natural world as a sphere of irrationality, animality and womanhood and with the withdrawal of men from the domestic sphere to the realm of public affairs ('civil society'). Primitivists, though no friend of Bookchin's, identify a similar process. Perlman describes the subjugation of women as the subjugation of Mother Earth and he counts the cost of the state's rise in terms of the destruction of biosphere. Government has its origins in God's instruction to the people of Israel to 'replenish the earth and subdue it, and have dominion over the fish of the sea, and over the fowl of the air, and over every living thing that moveth upon the earth'. The Bible suggests that this instruction was given first by God to Adam (Gen. 1: 28), but Perlman argues that Moses – the Lenin of the pre-Christian world – defined Leviathan's crusade. Either way, the message was a 'declaration of war against the Wilderness ... against all life'. Zerzan's explanation is that governmental forms of rule arose when human beings lost their 'awareness of belonging to an earthly community of living beings' and discovered a desire to domesticate ('bring under control for self-serving purposes') the natural world. Once humans had embarked on this process, the next step was to control and dominate each other through the habitual use of violence.

The material explanation of violence is that government must use coercive methods in order to maintain economic inequality. Anarchists are divided about the causes of inequality. Proudhon traced the roots of inequality to the right to property. However he distinguished between two types of right. The first was a right of dominion which allowed individuals to own property whether or not they occupied it and to derive rent, interest and profit from their ownership. This form of property was 'theft' and it contrasted with the second type of right, the right of ownership based on use or possession. These two forms of property were incompatible: the existence of one made the other 'impossible'. For example, if landowners were able to claim rights to collect rent from tenants, tenants had to give up their rights to their possessions in order to meet the demands. In Proudhon's view, the minority wielded economic power because the first form of property had been treated, wrongly, as an inalienable right. The recognition of this right, enshrined in liberal constitutions, gave an elite dominion over the land worked by the toilers.

Proudhon's theory supported the individualist idea that exploitation was based on monopoly rather than ownership itself and it contrasted with the communist theory advanced by Reclus, Kropotkin, Malatesta and others. They argued that economic inequality was in part caused by natural inequalities of talent and, in the other part, by the uneven quality of land and materials available to individuals. This analysis suggested that the right to property – even as possession – would always generate inequalities and, therefore, the existence of class division, supporting exploitation and government.

Both sides to this dispute agreed that economic inequality was a form of enslavement in which the propertyless mass was forced to work for the benefit of the owners. The choice was simple: either work on terms set by the owners or go without wages and the means of life. As Kropotkin noted, nobody freely consented to such an arrangement. Inequality could only be supported by coercion and deceit.

> ... how can the peasant be made to believe that the bourgeois or manorial land belongs to the proprietor who has a legal claim, when the peasant can tell us the history of each bit of land for ten leagues around? ... how make him believe that it is useful for the nation that Mr. So-and-so keeps a piece of land for his park when so many neighboring peasants would be only too glad to cultivate it?
>
> ... how make the worker in a factory, or the miner in a mine, believe that factory and mine equitably belong to their present masters, when worker and even miner are beginning to see clearly through scandal, bribery, pillage of the State and the legal theft, from which great commercial and industrial property are derived?[17]

Kropotkin also believed that inequalities between states explained the aggressiveness of the international system. Here the problem was that the most powerful industrialized European states competed with each other for markets, prestige and/or the control of raw materials. The system was inherently unstable. In Kropotkin's view, the 'reason for modern war is always the competition for markets and the right to exploit nations backward in industry'.[18]

Modern anarchists – though not anarcho-capitalists – continue to associate economic inequality with government violence. For example, the London Anarchist Communist Federation argue, '[t]he state is mainly a system of organized violence to maintain the domination of the capitalist ruling class. However, order is best achieved and maintained through people's consent rather than naked force'.[19] Yet modern anarchists are increasingly concerned with global inequality and the operation of international capitalism. Moreover, in their concern to look beyond the issue of class inequality, they tend to highlight the cultural and ecological impact of the global market economy – the destruction of traditional and indigenous cultures and the depletion of the earth's resources – rather than concentrate on its economic consequences. However, anti-capitalist theorists of globalization do not reject entirely the thrust of the traditional analyses of government. For example, Karen Goaman replicates the class divide that anarchists like Kropotkin posited between the propertyless mass and the owners in a division of global workers and multi-national corporations, the latter supported by states operating through international organizations like the World Trade Organization (WTO), the International Monetary Fund (IMF), The European Union (EU) and the World Bank. Her view is that

> Globalisation is the final drive for the control of the world's peoples and 'resources'. As a system based on competition, rapid change and the pursuit of profit through a particular set of social relationships based on wage labour (people with no other access to livelihood than to sell their labour) and machinery, it is predicated on the destruction of the commons, expansion and search for new markets, cheaper labour and ready access to the earth's (finite) riches.

Like the earlier forms of inequality, global capitalism breeds violence. Goaman continues:

> The difference between those processes as they affected us in the period from the 18th–20th centuries, and those carried out by world

leaders and those in the 'driving seat' of the globalisation process, lies in the massive amount of power now held by both states and corporations, particularly those in the US and the West, and all backed up by advanced technologies of repression, coercion and weapons of mass destruction.[20]

Some anarchists – Nicolas Walter, for example – acknowledge that 'every normal person would prefer to live under a less authoritarian rather than a more authoritarian' government.[21] Yet anarchist critiques of government violence tend to encourage anarchists to blur the differences, sometimes to the point of blindness, between forms of government and to discount consideration of the motivations or consequences of government action in favour of prioritizing the analysis of means. Arguments like Chomsky's reinforce the idea that the difference between constitutional and democratic governments, on the one hand, and tyrannies, on the other, is only a matter of degree. A familiar cry of anarchist pamphlets is that governments pay lip service to human rights in order to legitimize external aggression and exploitation, just as they use welfare and democracy as instruments of internal coercion. The critique has had two lasting effects on anarchist practice. The first is on the identification of anarchist sites of struggle. The only campaigns with which anarchists readily identify are those based on grass roots rebellion – for example, the struggles of Palestinians in the Occupied Territories and of Zapatistas in Mexico. Kropotkin's decision to support the Franco-British war effort in 1914 was the exception to prove the rule: since his action, the idea that anarchists might involve themselves in disputes between states is treated as anathema. Equally abhorrent is the idea that anarchists might attempt to harness the power of the state to ameliorate the effects of the free market. This rejection of the state is one of the hallmarks of anarchist anti-globalization protest. One voice puts the view succinctly:

> Too much of the time anti-globalization amounts to an appeal to the state to take account of the wishes of some of its 'citizens' and return to the good old days of social democracy and national sovereignty when the nation state protected us against the worst excesses of the corporations ... these sort of calls and complaints are quite simply reactionary ... states and governments are complicit in the process of globalization. We should understand this and act accordingly.[22]

The second practical effect of the critique concerns the permissible means of anarchist change. Here, anarchists are divided into two camps. On the one hand stand those who argue that change can only be won through non-violent methods. On the other are those who contend that organized violence can only be destroyed by violence. This division will be discussed in Chapter 4. The more immediate issue to consider is how anarchists explain the success of government. The answer, in large part, lies in their conceptions of authority.

authority and the state

If government describes the mechanism of the state's rule, authority is the principle that legitimizes the capacity to rule. According to Bakunin:

> Every logical and sincere theory of the State is essentially founded on the principle of *authority* – that is to say on the ... idea that the masses, *always* incapable of governing themselves, must submit at all times to the benevolent yoke of a wisdom and a justice, which one way or another, is imposed on them from above ... .[23]

Anarchist conceptions of state authority centre on three ideas: that authority is commanding, controlling and corrupting. Anarchists tend to discuss these ideas critically, linking command to the suspension of reason ('private judgement'); control to the stifling of initiative and creativity; and corruption to the inhibition of harmonious social relations.

The first idea, that authority is incompatible with private judgement, was at the heart of Godwin's anarchism. It also formed the core of Robert Paul Wolff's essay, *In Defence of Anarchism*. Wolff characterized the authority of the state as 'the *right* to command' and the 'correlative obligation *to obey the person who issues the command*'. When subject to authority individuals behave in certain ways not because they believe them to be justified or right, but merely because they have been commanded to do them. The exercise of authority 'is not a matter of doing what someone tells you to do. It is a matter of doing what he tells you to do *because he tells you to do it*'. Wolff contrasted authority with autonomy: the 'freedom and responsibility' that define dignified human behaviour. Autonomy allows individuals to do what others tell them to do, but only because they have made a judgement about the rightness of the instruction, and not because they are commanded to do it. Running these ideas together, Wolff argued that authority was incompatible with autonomy. Because he also held that individuals had a duty to be autonomous, he concluded that the concept of a legitimate state was a contradiction in terms.[24] Wolff's argument about the duty to be autonomous has been widely disputed. Yet his main point – that command is incompatible with reason and that the state, by inhibiting individuals from acting in accordance with their conscience and stripping them of responsibility for the choices and judgements they make – holds whether or not individuals are said to have this duty. And though Wolff's position was strictly philosophical, his critique of state authority has a broad appeal. As Emma Goldman argued '[a]narchism urges man to think, to investigate, to analyze every proposition'. The authority of the state prohibits and frustrates this endeavour. Similarly Rand argued:

> A rational mind does not work under compulsion; it does not subordinate its grasp of reality to anyone's orders, directives, or controls; it does not sacrifice its knowledge, its view of the truth, to anyone's opinions, threats, wishes, plans, or 'welfare'.[25]

In sum: anarchists since Godwin have complained that state authority forces individuals to do things they believe to be wrong and commands them to do things that they might otherwise agree to do. It not only makes hypocrites of its citizens but infantilizes them in the process.

The second critique, that authority stifles creativity, has two dimensions. Both focus on the notion of individuality, but one critique is concerned with issues of dependency whilst the other examines questions of expression. Falling into the first category, Kropotkin understood the problem of individuality as a problem of 'free initiative and free agreement'. In his view, the exercise of state authority – reinforced by the Church – had so disciplined and organized individuals that they had lost the habit of acting for themselves. The state had become 'the master of all the domains of human activity'. Individuals had little sense that they were independent beings, and still less that they could co-operate interdependently to achieve common goals. In response to the critics of anarchism who argued that authority was necessary to secure order, Kropotkin replied:

> We are told we are too slavish, too snobbish, to be placed under free institutions; but we say that because we are indeed so slavish we

ought not to remain any longer under the present institutions, which favour the development of slavishness.[26]

In recent years Kropotkin's critique has been revived by social anarchists – amongst others – interested in stimulating grassroots, community initiatives designed to bypass the authority of the state. However, many anarchists – particularly modern anarchists – are as exercised with the issue of expression as they are the problem of dependency. From this perspective authority is linked to the inculcation of moral values and behavioural norms. It is said to inhibit individuals from exploring their uniqueness and to mould them in ways that make them more likely to conform to the state's commands. This understanding of authority draws on a number of sources, notably Stirner, Nietzsche (notwithstanding Nietzsche's dismissal of anarchism as a moralizing creed) and the Situationist International (SI). For example, Daniel Guérin turned to Stirner to appeal against conformity with family values and, more specifically, to resist the homophobic and repressive sexual morality of bourgeois rule. The feminist Dora Marsden also drew on Stirner's work to assert her continuous rebellion against all standards of thought and behaviour. By authority she understood the desire to categorize thought and purpose through the imposition of abstract ideas – 'society', 'community', 'property', even 'anarchy'. Her anti-authoritarian creative urge was a refusal to sacrifice her individual rebelliousness to any of the common causes these categories expressed. Consequently, Marsden distinguished the 'phenomenal advance' that individual women had made in liberating themselves from categories like 'woman' from the 'stationaryness and ... stagnation' of the 'Woman Movement'. The first was driven forward by the energy of separate egos. The latter by an authority that sapped those 'streams of living energy'. In her view, the important lesson taught by anarchism was that 'individual soul's development' was 'the supreme concern of its possessor'.[27]

Anarchist Nietzscheans include writers as different as Emma Goldman and Herbert Read. Goldman's account of the battle against authority was that it was a battle against 'uniformity' and public opinion, not just oppression or persecution. For Read, Nietzsche had importantly defined the individual as 'a world in himself, self-contained and self-creative', a 'freely giving and freely receiving, but essentially a free spirit'.[28] Though Read believed that Nietzsche had not clearly understood how individuals could live together creatively, he argued that he had been right to conceive the struggle against authority as an existential revolt. Read thus endorsed Albert Camus' characterization of the modern struggle as a 'metaphysical revolt, the revolt of man against the conditions of life, against creation itself'.[29]

Anarchists drawing inspiration from the SI include insurrectionists like Alfredo Bonanno, postmoderns and primitivists. Taking up some of the ideas of the SI anarchists have attempted to show how the structures of the state hinder expression, or what surrealists term the realization of 'the Marvelous'. As Zerzan explains, the contribution of the SI lies particularly in the notion of the spectacle and in the analysis of the commodity-developed world. Individuals, in what Zerzan pejoratively calls 'civilization' or 'symbolic culture', understand the world indirectly, 'by blocking and otherwise suppressing channels of sensory awareness'. Technology compels them 'to tune out' most of what they could otherwise experience. Life is drained of real meaning and '[m]assive, unfulfilling consumption … reigns as the chief everyday consolation'. In the 'horror-show of domination' people relate to each other through 'entertaining, easily digestible images and phrases'. They become illiterate and fatalistic, 'indifferent to questions of origins, agency, history or causation'.[30] Too many estimate their own worth by the standards of the perfect consumer goods that surround them. Some, as Nicki Clarke suggests, become self-haters: 'I'm starving myself, watching my breasts and hips disappear – you know I understand the hatred of this body, this sexualised body, this packaged consumerproductbody that exists for someone else's enjoyment, someone else's eye. Not mine.'[31] Others are driven to insanity. Alfredo Bonanno picks up the story. Individuals who manage to escape 'the commodity code' and fall '"outside" the areas of the spectacle … are pointed at. They are surrounded by barbed wire … they are criminalized. They are clearly mad!' He continues: 'It is forbidden to refuse the illusory in a world that has based reality on illusion, concreteness on the unreal'.[32]

The final critique, that authority is corrupting, focuses on the relational qualities of state rule. This critique is a complaint about the state's falsity and the way in which it stirs antagonism in society. Tolstoy's version of this thesis was based on a moral view, linked to his Christianity. He defined authority as 'the means of forcing a man to act contrary to his desires' and contrasted it to 'spiritual influence'. Authority, he argued, encouraged hypocrisy. In this context, hypocrisy is not merely about being forced to act against conscience

or to act in ways contrary to professed belief but, borrowing a theatrical metaphor, about playing a part and concealing true character.
Tolstoy's view was that authority did not just subject individuals to
command, but that the issuing of commands led them to think
and behave in ways that were alien and destructive. Authority
'hypnotized' individuals, convincing them 'that they are whatever
character is suggested to them'. When subject to authority individuals lose the 'power of reflecting on their actions' they 'do without
thinking whatever is consistent with the suggestion to which they are
led by example, precept, or insinuation'.

Notable hypocrites in the political system are heads of states,
military commanders and priests. But the hypocrites are not just the
figureheads or leaders in society or even those who occupy official
positions in the state – in the armed forces or police, for example.
Some anarchists are quick to condemn people in these positions.
After the London poll tax riot, one anarchist described the police as
'the first line of defence for the system' concluding that they 'deserve
everything they get'.[33] According to Tolstoy, however, hypocrisy has
'entered into the flesh and blood of all classes in our time'. Anyone
can be hypnotized to play a role by authority. Hypocrites not only
include regular soldiers who kill, maim and torture their fellow-
beings by order; but peasants and workers who meekly submit to
conscription; 'tradesmen, doctors, artists, clerks, scientists, cooks,
writers, valets, and lawyers' who wrongly assume that they occupy
benevolent or useful social roles. Hypocrites refuse to acknowledge
their roles. Indeed, hypocrisy is so deeply embedded in the state that
it is even possible, Tolstoy noted sourly, for a man to 'remain a
landowner, a trader, a manufacturer, a judge, an official in government pay, a soldier or an officer, and still be not merely humane but
even a socialist and a revolutionary'.[34]

Perlman shared Tolstoy's belief that authority structures social
relationships, but detached the analysis from spirituality. For
Perlman, authority was a form of ideology, in the sense in which
Jason McQuinn defines the term: a particular use of ideas, designed
'to subordinate and control' and involving 'the adoption of theories
constructed around abstract, externally-conceived subjectivities ...
to which one feels in some ways obliged to subordinate ... aims,
desires and life'.[35] In Perlman's account, individuals are not so much
corrupted by authority, but nevertheless manipulated and mentally
programmed as if hypnotized. In Leviathan's grip 'the individual's
living spirit shrivels and dies' and the 'empty space is filled ... with

Leviathan's substance'. Individuals become aggressive, anti-social beings. Leviathan's historic mission was 'to reduce human beings to things, to remake men into efficient fighting units'. And it succeeded in its task. Individuals had learned to experience joy 'from the fall of an enemy and the gushing of blood from a wound'. Drawing on theatrical metaphor, Perlman continued:

> ... the tragedy of it all is that the longer he wears the armor, the less able he is to remove it. The armor sticks to his body. The mask becomes glued to his face. Attempts to remove the mask become increasingly painful, for the skin tends to come off with it. There's still a human face below the mask, just as there's still a potentially free body below the armor, but merely airing them takes almost superhuman effort.[36]

Critics often claim that anarchists have an overly optimistic view of human nature. Yet Tolstoy's and Perlman's critiques of authority do not suggest that the individuals are naturally 'good'. They argue that the state has made us artificially 'bad'. What's the difference? From this perspective the problem of the state is not that it creates social conflicts, but that it habitually relies on violence to resolve differences. With its authority the state variously conditions individuals to follow instructions, encourages herd-like instincts and brutalizes citizens by moulding their responses to others. And how does authority work? The answer is: through power. As Rocker remarked, power 'is active consciousness of authority'. Anarchist analyses of power highlight the ways in which authority manifests itself in daily life.

power and the state

Anarchist analyses of power focus on the instruments that governments use to enforce authority. Some anarchists have understood these instruments to refer to the visible legal and political structures of physical repression. Others have looked at covert forces of control: the power of ideology – particularly nationalism – and, more recently, concepts like time, work and school.

The most obvious way in which the state uses power is through the legal system and its supporting institutions. Anarchists acknowledge that these systems and supports can be more or less developed and that the relationship between the machinery of law and the enforcing institutions is balanced in different ways. States governed by 'coercion' are more likely than those governed by 'deceit' to have very well-developed systems of enforcement and will rely more heavily on these systems to secure compliance than on the rule of law. In his classic analysis of the Okhrana, the Tsarist secret police, Victor Serge showed how the autocracy had employed a range of powers, from surveillance techniques to systematic execution and disappearance, to defend itself against revolution. In the inter-war period Alexander Berkman raised a similar case, this time showing how Tsarist methods had been imported into Bolshevism in defence of Lenin's revolution. The view famously developed by Proudhon is that these instruments of power are a necessary feature of all government:

> To be GOVERNED is to be kept in sight, inspected, spied upon, directed, law-driven, numbered, enrolled, indoctrinated, preached at, controlled, estimated, valued, censured, commanded ... to be GOVERNED is to be at every operation, at every transaction, noted, registered, enrolled, taxed, stamped, measured, numbered, assessed, licensed, authorized, admonished, forbidden, reformed, corrected, punished. It is ... to be placed under contribution, trained, ransomed, exploited, monopolized, extorted, squeezed, mystified, robbed ... to be repressed, fined, despised, harassed, tracked, abused, clubbed, disarmed, choked, imprisoned, judged, condemned, shot, deported, sacrificed, sold, betrayed; and, to crown it all, mocked, ridiculed, outraged, dishonoured.[37]

Tolstoy (who also borrowed from Proudhon the title of his masterwork, *War and Peace*) similarly emphasized the physical aspect of power.

> The possibility of exercising physical violence is given by organization of armed men, wherein all act in unison, submitting to one will. Such assemblies of armed men submitting to one will constitute the army. The army has always been and is still the basis of power. Power is always in the hands of those who command the army, therefore all rulers, from Roman Caesars to German and Russian Emperors, are engrossed in cares for the army, whom they flatter and cajole, for they know that if the army is with them, power also is in their hands.[38]

Altering the focus of discussion, Kropotkin identified law as one of the most effective instruments of government power. His attack on law consisted of three claims: that the law had been imposed, that it discouraged social experimentation and that it was dehumanizing. The first claim was directed against liberals who argued that the origins of law lay in agreement, and conservatives who suggested that it was the result of an organic process of development. Both were wrong. The law, Kropotkin argued, was 'a product of modern times' and of modern civilization. It was introduced to replace those 'customs, habits and usages' that once regulated human relations in Europe and which continued to do so in other geographical areas. Its introduction, though presented as a social achievement, was in fact the result of the cynical manipulation of the people by the ruling class. Law, Kropotkin argued, originated in the desire of the 'ruling class to give permanence to customs imposed by themselves for their own advantage'.

Kropotkin's second claim was that law regimented human life and inhibited innovation. Law was an efficient instrument of change, but not necessarily an effective one. Law-makers legislated without knowing what their laws were about. For example, they passed laws 'on the sanitation of towns, without the faintest notion of hygiene'; they made 'regulations for the armament of troops, without so much as understanding a gun'; and they made laws 'about teaching and education without ever having given a lesson of any sort, or even an honest education to their own children'. Moreover, whilst legislators failed to improve social conditions, the law stifled efforts to initiate real reform from below. Echoing his critique of authority, Kropotkin argued that any residual enthusiasm that individuals in the state nurtured for social change or improvement was dampened by the prospect of having to jump through endless legal hoops. Under law, Kropotkin concluded, society was characterized by the 'spirit of routine … indolence, and cowardice'.

Kropotkin's final charge, that the law was alienating and dehumanizing, was based on his understanding of the corrupting tendency of power. The corruption Kropotkin associated with the law was not the power to abuse legislative responsibility – as liberal critics feared – but the tendency to encourage mistrust, suspicion and vindictiveness in the individuals who were caught up in its systems of enforcement. Law required regiments of people to staff its offices and encouraged in them the most abject behaviour. Amongst the law enforcers was the 'detective trained as a blood-hound, the police spy despising himself'. In the law, Kropotkin continued, informing, was 'metamorphosed into a virtue; corruption, effected into a system. All 'the vices, all the evil qualities of mankind' were 'countenanced and cultivated to insure the triumph of law'.[39]

For anarchists like Kropotkin, the power of the state was something that could be seen in its institutions – police stations, law courts and prisons – and in the observable behaviour of those ruled by them. Developing a slightly different approach, some anarchists have defined the power of the state as the ability to manipulate. These anarchists do not deny that power changes the way in which people behave, but find power located in invisible sources. For example, writing in the inter-war period Rudolf Rocker identified nationalism as a source of manipulation. He traced the roots of nationalism to the early-nineteenth-century patriotism and, in particular, to Guiseppe Mazzini's romantic aspirations for Italian unity. Patriotism was inspired by a 'sincere love of the people' and sprang from a genuine desire to achieve social unity through emancipation. But it was undermined by the patriots' misconception that the state was the proper vehicle for the achievement of solidarity. As a result it gave way to late or modern nationalism, which was entirely manipulative, 'wholly lacking in … love' and 'genuine feeling'. Nationalism was a vehicle for a particular philosophy of the state that Rocker identified with the Italian Hegelian, Giovanni Gentile. Gentile's idea was that the state had an ethical character. It was the instrument through which humanity realized its potential, bringing disparate individuals together in community, and it was an expression of human reason. And it achieved this end by imposing uniformity and legitimizing the state's domination of every field of human activity: the arts, religion, philosophy and morality. Mussolini, Hitler and Stalin eagerly applied Gentile's ideas.

> Modern nationalism is only will-toward-the-state-at-any-price and complete absorption of man in the higher ends of power … modern nationalism has its roots in the ambitious plans of a minority lusting for dictatorship and determined to impose upon the people a certain form of state …[40]

Fredy Perlman's critique of nationalism picks up some of Rocker's themes. In his view nationalism is a dynamic process of state formation which has its roots in the American and French revolutions. Like Rocker, Perlman associated nationalism with militarism and argued that both fascism and Bolshevism were exemplars of nationalist ideology. The heirs of Lenin, Perlman argued, were people 'like Mussolini … and Hitler, people who, like Lenin himself, cursed their weak and inept bourgeoisies for having failed to establish their nation's greatness'. Yet in contrast to Rocker, Perlman argued that nationalism predated the idea of the nation. On his account nationalism was never about patriotic self-determination or emancipation, but always about domination and control. To those who defined the nation as 'an organized territory consisting of people who share a common language, religion and customs', Perlman argued:

> This is not a description of the phenomenon but an apology for it, a justification … The common language, religion and customs … were mere pretexts, instruments for mobilizing armies. The culmination of the process was not an enshrinement of the commonalities, but a depletion, a total loss of language, religion and customs; the inhabitants of a nation … worshipped on the altar of the state and confined their customs to those permitted by the national police.[41]

Perlman's conclusion, like Rocker's, was that nationalism served only to draw the people closer to Leviathan and that its success could be measured by their willingness to regard others with hostility as outsiders.

Rather than concentrating on nationalism, other primitivists have identified the power of the state with what appear to be the blander – but also more insidious – aspects of ideology. For example, one of Zerzan's concerns is the notion of time. In 1944 George Woodcock wrote an essay denouncing as a tyrannous abstraction the domination of mechanized time. Zerzan develops a similar view, comparing linear to cyclical time. Linear time orders and constrains us by structuring our activities – in the workplace, forcing the pace of production and organizing the routine of daily life – and our consciousness. It has no connection with the rhythms of the natural world. In linear time life is understood as a simple progression in which each individual waits for its end. It is the measure of 'history, then progress, then an idolatry of the future that sacrifices species, languages, cultures, and … the entire natural world on the altar of some future'.[42]

The anti-anarchist Bob Black attacks the idea of work which, drawing on the thought of the French philosopher Michel Foucault, he equates with discipline. Work, he argues, is a site for 'totalitarian' control: 'surveillance, rotework, imposed work tempos, production quotas, punching-in and -out'.[43] In Black's view, workplaces – factories, offices and shops – are no different in kind from prisons, though they have a different ambience. Work might not be as regimented as prison life, but it is imposed like a prison sentence and workers believe it to be necessary and willingly spend the best part of their lives in burdensome jobs that turn them into automata. Black does not suppose that work, any more than time, has been created by the state. What he argues is that work is something that has arisen with the state's development. And like other ideologies, work is considered a form of state power because it helps to maintain a condition that the state uses to justify its own existence. Most important, work supports and is supported by education or, as Zerzan defines it, 'knowledge production'. In schools, children learn 'that they are always being observed, monitored and evaluated'.[44] The apparent blandness of ideology thus describes the insidiousness of the state's command of daily life.

Returning to Rocker's remark that power 'is active consciousness of authority', the table below summarizes the ways in which Kropotkin, Tolstoy, Zerzan and Perlman have encapsulated this relationship.

Anarchist Conceptions of Authority and Power

	Kropotkin	Tolstoy	Zerzan	Perlman
Authority	Dependency	Hypocrisy/ hypnosis	Commodification/ objectification	Psychological /cultural repression
Power	Law	Armed force	Ideological abstraction	Nationalism

Though anarchists have defined power and authority – and the violence it supports – differently, the relationship that anarchists posit between this triad forms the bedrock of their critiques of the state. The next section considers why anarchists reject the state: the first looks at the negativity of the state, and the second at its redundancy.

anarchist critiques of the state

It is possible to draw some of the grounds of the anarchists' objections to the state from their definitions of government, authority and power. For example, anarchists variously claim that the state is immoral (breeding violence and aggression), repressive (stifling creativity), and inefficient (dampening local initiative). Anarchists have used all and any of these complaints to call for the state's abolition. But perhaps the most persistent complaint is that the state is unjust. This claim turns on the charge that the state exists to maintain inequality and it has two aspects. Some anarchists argue that the state is exploitative, others that it is alienating.

The idea that the state is an instrument of exploitation has two variants. The first, associated with individualists like Rothbard, is based on the coercive and parasitical nature of the state's relationship with its citizens. According to this view, the state is a 'vast engine of insitutionalized crime' that steals property from individuals by threat of aggression. It's a racket, little different from the Mafia. The second view, advanced by anarcho-communists and anarcho-syndicalists, extends from the observation of the class inequalities that government defends. In Kropotkin's words, exploitation divides 'mankind into two camps; the poor on the one side and on the other the idlers and the playboys with their fine worlds and brutal appetites'.[45] The London Anarchist Communist Federation provide a more recent account:

> Though capitalism is a global system of exploitation and banditry with huge multinational companies operating everywhere, the basis of it is quite simple. Basically, wealth is created by people who use tools to adapt the raw materials provided by nature. In order to survive, workers are forced to sell their labour ('wage slavery') at the market price. In their work, workers make the goods which are part of everyday life and provide services. However, the rewards workers receive in the form of wages are less than the value of the products and services they bring about.[46]

On this understanding, exploitation is not straightforward extortion, as Rothbard would have it, but a form of cheating. Capitalists employ workers to produce goods that they can sell at a profit. To do this, they invent ways of lowering their production costs and maximizing worker productivity. Thus exploitation involves, on the one hand, low wages, investment in areas where labour is cheapest and deskilling ('the McDonaldization of labour') and, on the other, the mechanization of production, shift systems, the division of labour and the strict scheduling of production tasks ('Taylorism'). In addition, anarcho-syndicalists associate exploitation with a set of managerial and political structures. A SolFed pamphlet argues:

> Capitalism, where profit takes precedence over everything else, is the heart of the problem ... A tiny number of capitalists exert real power through their ownership and control of the economy. Our basic rights to a decent life are dependent on our ability to generate income.
>
> It is the few who decide who gets to work for these basic rights and who doesn't. It is the few who do the hiring and firing, and determine the conditions in which we are forced to work ...
>
> With the excess profits they get from our work, capitalists have undisputed economic power ...
>
> ... it is the nature of capitalism which makes people 'have to' act in their interest and against other's and the environment. It's not a few bad people, it's a bad system. Capitalism concentrates power – in political parties, in company and state hierarchies. All this leads to misuse, mistrust and abuse.[47]

Anarcho-communists and anarcho-syndicalists argue that exploitation affects the quality of social relations. It undermines co-operation and encourages competition between workers, thus breeding mistrust. Workers become prey to 'false divisions' – manipulated by sexist, racist and homophobic ideas. Disunited, workers feel isolated and insecure.

Alienation is a theme linked to post-Situationist anarchism and has been explored by writers including Perlman and Zerzan. Though it is linked to exploitation, in their hands it describes the impact that the production process – and the technology it supports – has on individuals rather than the mechanisms through which capitalists make their profits. Perlman described alienation in terms of 'reproduction'. He argued that the principle of reproduction is the same in all types of economy – so reproduction in slavery is not very different from capitalist reproduction. In the former, slaves reproduce 'the instruments with which the master represses them, and their own habits of submission to the master's authority'. In the latter, wage-labourers 'reproduce ... the social relations and the ideas of their society; they reproduce the social form of daily life'.[48] In both cases the essence of reproduction is that it perpetuates forms of cultural or psychological domination. As Perlman argues: 'compulsive and compulsory reproduction' is responsible for the 'cadaver's life'.

Leviathan, he notes elsewhere, is 'an excretion' of the reproductive process. The exploited are alienated because they spend their time recreating the complex social, economic and political structures responsible for their domination and oppression.

Zerzan develops his view of alienation from Marx but suggests that Marx defined the concept too narrowly as a 'separation' from the means of production. Being alienated, Zerzan argues, means being 'estranged from our own experiences, dislodged from a natural mode of being'. Like Perlman, Zerzan argues that exploitation lies at the heart of alienation because it has brought into being a colossal industrial system that forces individuals to regard the world as an object of consumption. Dependent on industrial technology to provide for their wants, people destroy the only thing that they really need: the natural world. In America the effect has been to create a 'jarring contrast between reality and what is said about reality'. People are encouraged to think in terms of 'dreams' but are frustrated by the impossibility of their achievement. The 'nightmare scenario' is that the

> contrast can go on forever: people ... won't even notice there's no natural world anymore, no freedom, no fulfilment, no nothing. You just take your Prozac everyday, limp along dyspeptic and neurotic, and figure that's all there is.[49]

The scenario, Zerzan argues, is aptly captured in Ted Kaczynski's *Unabomber Manifesto*. Kaczynski distinguishes between three 'human drives' – those that can be satisfied 'with minimal effort', those that can be satisfied 'at the cost of serious effort', and those that cannot be 'adequately satisfied no matter how much effort one makes'. In a healthy society, human drives are channelled into the second group: individuals must make some effort to secure their physical and social needs. Modern industrial society pushes these drives into the 'first and third groups'. Physical necessities are provided with minimal effort and, to compensate for the loss, the market invents artificial needs which 'modern man' [sic] feels obliged but unable to satisfy. The result is a profound sense of 'purposelessness'.[50]

These critiques of exploitation and alienation provide an important bridge between anarchism and non-anarchist schools of socialism. The strength of the anarchists' commitment to end state exploitation and put an end to alienation is acknowledged by non-anarchists to play an important part in contemporary protest. As Michael Albert argues, anarchists 'fight on the side of the oppressed in every domain of life, from family, to culture, to state, to economy ... and ... do so in creative and courageous ways ...'.[51] Yet non-anarchists have long argued that the anarchists' rejection of government, authority and power raise difficult questions about the functioning of anarchy and its realization. How can people co-operate in the absence of rules? How can individuals enter into agreements with others if they refuse to be bound by authority? How can they realize their aims without exercising power? Closer inspection of anarchist thought provides some answers to these questions and suggests that the anarchists' rejections of government, authority and power are misleading. For the most part, anarchist theories indicate that some forms of government, authority and power can be legitimated. What they deny is that these legitimate forms can flourish in the state.

self-government, 'natural' authority and 'social' power

In response to their critics, anarchists demonstrate the redundancy of the state by showing how systems of government and authority can be incorporated into anarchy in a manner that provides social order without repression, uniformity or social division. In addition, they argue that the locus of power distinguishes its legitimate from its illegitimate exercise.

anarchism and government

The incorporation of government into anarchy rests on a distinction between government and self-government. Anarchists have interpreted this distinction in myriad ways. Kropotkin's version was grounded on the suggestion, developed through his critique of Marxism, that government could be abstracted from the state. Kropotkin's argument was that Marxists had wrongly defined both government and state in terms of class. As a result, they had adopted a too narrow view of revolutionary change and limited their ambitions to the alteration of the government's class character. In his essay *The State: Its Historic Role* Kropotkin argued:

> It seems to me ... that State and government represent two ideas of a different kind. The State not only includes the existence of a

power placed above society, but also a *territorial concentration and a concentration of many or even all functions of the life of society in the hands of a few*. It implies new relations among the members of society.[52]

Malatesta took up the point. The word 'state', he argued, referred to

> ... the impersonal, abstract expression of that state of affairs
> personified by government: and therefore the terms abolition
> of the State, Society without the State, etc., describe exactly the
> concept which anarchists seek to express, of the destruction of all
> political order based on authority, and the creation of a society
> of free and equal members based on a harmony of interests and
> the voluntary participation of everybody in carrying out social
> responsibilities.[53]

Whereas the state described the framework within which government operated, government described a transitory set of political arrangements that could take a number of different forms – democratic, monarchical, aristocratic and so forth. Admittedly, the state coloured the operation of all the forms of government functioning within it. Nevertheless, it was possible to imagine forms of government without the state. Kropotkin supported this suggestion with a historical analysis of the state's rise, which he located between the twelfth and fifteenth centuries in the collapse of the medieval city-states, the concentration of monarchical power in newly centralized governing institutions and the rise of capitalism. Kropotkin did not suggest that the medieval cities were anarchies. Indeed he classified them as states. Nonetheless, he argued that they differed fundamentally from modern states. The 'essential point' about them was that the inhabitants had jurisdiction over their own affairs. In contrast to the modern state, power was not concentrated but dispersed through systems of self-administration. Though these systems ultimately failed, they nevertheless demonstrated the possibility of self-government.

In the 1960s and '70s, anarchists excited about cybernetics (the study of communication and control mechanisms, primarily in machines, but also in living things) found the distinction between illegitimate and legitimate government in the concept 'self-organization'. In contrast to government control mechanisms, self-organizing systems were controlled from within the organism and could respond to their ever-changing diversity. As

John McEwan argued, the latter were potential models for anarchist organization:

> The basic premise of the governmentalist – namely, that any society must incorporate some mechanism for overall control – is certainly true … The error of the governmentalist is to think that 'incorporate some mechanism for control' is always equivalent to 'include a fixed isolatable control unit to which the rest, *i.e.* the majority, of the system is subservient'. This may be an adequate interpretation in the case of a model railway system, but not for a human society.[54]

To give a final example: modern Kropotkinites have captured the distinction between government and self-government by contrasting two understandings of the word 'rule'. In the *Bulletin of the Anarchist International* Scandinavian anarchists argue that one is referring to the settlement of disputes 'in an orderly way' and the other to 'regulation'. The English language, they continue, has only one word to describe these ideas. As a consequence, anarchists have wrongly been encouraged to consider both illegitimate. In their view, the English standard must be rejected in favour of the Scandinavian language model, which captures these different meanings in separate words. Anarchism, they believe, is open to the first idea of 'rule' and closed only to the idea of regulation.

anarchism and authority

The possibility of incorporating authority into an anarchist framework turns on the distinctions anarchists sometimes draw between types of authority. There are two strands to the arguments. The first is based on a distinction between being *in* and being *an* authority, and the second between natural and artificial authority.

In the first instance, anarchists classically associate 'in' authority with the authority of the state. As Jeremy Westall writes: to be '*in* authority is to have powers of coercion'. Being an authority can mean a variety of things. Westall's idea is that it describes a form of advice. A person with authority is 'a person who is competent and well versed in a specific subject'.[55] Bakunin, however, identified legitimate authority with instruction as well as advice. In a discussion of education he argued that 'authority… is legitimate, necessary when applied to children of a tender age, whose intelligence has not yet openly developed itself'. Its purpose was 'the formation of free men full of respect and love for the liberty of others'. On advice, the general rule was that:

> In the matter of boots I refer to the authority of the bootmakers; concerning houses, canals, or railroads I consult that of the architect or engineer. For such or such special knowledge I apply to such or such a *savant*. But I allow neither the bootmaker nor the architect nor the *savant* to impose his authority upon me. I accept them freely and with all the respect merited by their intelligence, their character, their knowledge, reserving always my incontestable right of criticism and censure.[56]

Bakunin was aware that legitimate authority could always degenerate into an illegitimate form. He was particularly critical of the authoritative rulings of scientists and although he celebrated the application of scientific knowledge to alleviate suffering and improve the condition of human life, he so feared the possibility that scientists might abuse their capacity to advise, that he declared himself to be in revolt against the 'government of science'.

The second distinction, between natural and artificial forms of authority, is perhaps the most important, for it establishes the basis on which anarchists ground compliance to voluntary agreements. The distinctive feature of natural authority is that it is deemed to be internal or to issue from below rather than from the command of an external body. Anarchists have described this kind of authority in different ways. To the disgust of anarcha-feminists Proudhon contrasted the legitimacy of patriarchal authority in the family with the illegitimate political authority in the state. Bakunin distinguished 'the divine, theological, metaphysical, political, and judicial authorities, established by the Church, and by the State' from the 'natural and rational', 'wholly human' authority of the 'collective and public spirit of a society founded on the mutual respect of its members'. This authority sprang from the 'natural and inevitable' sense of solidarity that held society together. It commanded respect and ensured compliance with social rules. Yet it could not enslave since it was not imposed 'from without'. Herbert Read distinguished between 'a discipline imposed on life, and the law which is inherent to life'. Drawing on his wartime experiences, he exemplified the first in 'mechanical routine of the barrack square' and associated the second with the 'tyranny' of the 'law of nature'.[57]

Similar distinctions can be found in new anarchist schools of thought. Admittedly, primitivists tend to be more concerned to investigate the reasons why authority has become necessary than they are with analysing the ways in which anarchists might secure compliance. Moreover, they are extremely critical of those 'old' anarchists who have sought to find alternatives to state authority without questioning the conditions – industrial technology, work and the division of labour – deemed responsible for bringing this authority into being. Nevertheless, primitivist writings support an idea of authority as self-regulation. Perlman contrasts the 'voice of Leviathan' which 'speaks of Commandments and Punishments' to the voice of Nature that 'speaks of ways, of paths to Being'. Leviathan has 'laws ... closed gates' and says: 'Thou shalt not'. In contrast Nature springs from an 'inner voice' and says: 'Thou canst and Thou shalt Be'. Leviathan is disciplining, Nature enabling.[58] Some primitivists prefer to distinguish between government authority and persuasion. In a variation on this theme Zerzan contrasts persuasion to domination. Like legitimate authority, persuasion requires that individuals comply with certain internally imposed standards of behaviour. Above all it requires them to be honest and to refuse the opportunity to manipulate others to achieve personal goals.

In whichever way anarchists choose to describe the idea, 'authority from below' enables them to distinguish between types of commitment and to argue that anarchism is consistent with some forms of binding agreement. Specifically, it allows them to reject as artificial the authority of the state on the grounds that it forces individuals to uphold agreements that have not been entered into freely, but to defend the naturalness of promising. Like commands, promises create obligations that individuals must respect. Once a promise has been made, individuals are expected to place it beyond review. Yet, unlike commands, the binding obligations that promises create are legitimate, because promises are made voluntarily. The important point here, as Proudhon argued, is that promising is an expression of natural authority and it provides a basis for social order in anarchy.

> Do you promise to respect the honour, the liberty and the property of your brothers?
>
> Do you promise never to appropriate for yourself by violence, nor by fraud, nor by usury, nor by interest, the products or possessions of another?
>
> Do you promise never to lie nor to deceive in commerce, or in any of your transactions?

You are free to accept or refuse.

If you refuse, you become a part of a society of savages. Excluded from communion with the human race, you become an object of suspicion. Nothing protects you ...

If you agree to the compact, on the contrary, you become a part of the society of free men. All your brothers are bound to you, and promise you fidelity, friendship, aid, service, exchange.[59]

A notable objection to this position comes from Stirnerites like Dora Marsden. In a bad-tempered dispute with Benjamin Tucker about Proudhon, she denounced the idea of voluntary contract as impossible and dangerous and contrasted the anarchist vision of society to her own ideal, the union of egoists. Probably more anarchists align themselves with Proudhon than Marsden on this issue. And whether or not they like to identify anarchy with authority, some version of the idea usually underpins the concepts of trust, mutual support, voluntary co-operation – and, indeed, liberty – commonly identified with this order.

anarchism and power

Anarchists usually understand power to encompass a range of actions, from physical coercion to influence and persuasion and that it can be exercised both openly and in covert ways. Some anarchists suggest that power is a possession of individuals. Even if it happens to be exercised through the institutions of government, power is associated with the people who run those institutions rather than being vested in the institutions themselves. Other anarchists argue that power is best seen as a feature of the social system or structure. From this point of view, power is not wielded by individuals, but is something that permeates the institutions they inhabit. Anarchists who adopt the first view include anarcho-communists and anarcho-syndicalists, who condemn the state on the grounds of exploitation, and primitivists and others who associate the state with alienation. Those who adopt the second veer towards postmodern/poststructuralist anarchism.

Anarchists have developed their ideas of power with reference to the state's abolition, transcendence or destruction. Because they regard the nature of government in different ways, they also disagree about power and its legitimate use. Emphasizing the exploitative function of the state, anarcho-communists and syndicalists tend to identify the legitimate use of power with the collective or combined force of the oppressed. Primitivists, on the other hand, complement their view of state alienation with a view that power is legitimate only when exercised by the individual. The postmodern view is that power has no real centre and that, rather than being possessed by collectives or individuals, it permeates social relationships. From this perspective, power can manifest itself in positive and negative ways, but cannot be captured in legitimate or illegitimate spheres.

As representatives of the first view, Rocker and Kropotkin imagined that the abolition of power would be achieved through the expropriation of private property and the realization of common ownership by the movement of workers and peasants. The state, Kropotkin argued, would be abolished when 'the workers in the factories and the cultivators in the fields march hand in hand to the conquest of equality for all'. Indeed, Kropotkin argued that 'in the task of reconstructing society on new principles, separate men, however intelligent and devoted they may be' were sure to fail. He continued: '[t]he collective spirit of the masses is necessary for this purpose'.[60] Rocker's syndicalist idea was that the struggle against the state 'must take the form of ... the solidaric [sic] collaboration of the workers ... through taking over the management of all plants by the producers themselves ...'.[61] Modern anarcho-syndicalists similarly discuss the necessity of developing a 'culture of solidarity', of creating 'a new ... sense of community through the practice of solidarity'.

Primitivists do not deny the important role that mass actions might have in undermining the state, but shy away from the idea that individuals might be made subject to collective force. Zerzan advocates wildcat strikes and factory occupations on the model of the May 1968 uprising in France, political vandalism, roaming riots and militant protest. However, unlike Kropotkin, his ambition is not to organize workers to expropriate owners and dismantle the means of industrial production. It is to encourage each individual – separately – to engage in the struggle against the 'domination of nature, subjugation of women, war, religion ... and division of labor'. United, mass actions emerge from the impulse to individual rebellion. John Moore offered a similar view. He argued that the struggle against the state should be waged by individuals, communicating through the arts – particularly poetry. His hope was that anarchists would be able to touch popular passions and irrationalities, reach out and communicate with others and 'realize' and 'supercede' the arts beyond their 'alienated and commodified' form. The struggle would involve many people. But Moore's underlying conviction was that it was a self-creative revolt, taking '*radical subjectivity* as the basis for resistance'. It was about 'the subject-in-process ... the subject-in-rebellion'.[62] Elsewhere, Moore argued that struggle was about the possibility of 'becoming' and 'the emancipation of life from governance and control' by the 'exploration of desire and the free, joyful pursuit of individual lines of interest'.[63] Either way, it was not really about solidarity or collective action.

This idea of individual struggle bears some similarity to the libertarian anarchist position. One of Rand's great cries is that rational individuals ought not be made subject to the actions of collectives. However, there is an important difference between the two positions. Whereas primitivists like Moore adopt an expansive view of the individual, Rand takes an insular view. For her, struggle is not about becoming, it's about securing a realm of action for the individual, free from interference. To this extent, Moore's position has more in common with Read's or Tolstoy's than it does with Rand's. Indeed, though their work had a spiritual dimension which Moore's lacks, they shared his belief that struggle was about regeneration and that art was a touchstone for awakening the unconscious.

The – postmodern – view also has something in common with the primitivist position. Like primitivists, postmodern anarchists identify struggle with notions of becoming, with creativity and expression. For postmodern anarchists, however, struggle is a continual process that is not so much focused on the individual as it is on networks of individuals and their movements. The dominant image – borrowed from the French philosophers, Giles Deleuze and Felix Guattari – is of the rhizome: a root which sends out shoots in different directions and which connects with others in complex and unpredictable ways. The rhizome describes the nature of human interactions and it suggests that struggle is not about breaking free from constraints, but about defining identity and discovering diversity within the root system.

Some anarchists – Moore was not amongst them – are prepared to define their approach to the state's abolition in terms of a conception of power. For example, Bakunin identified solidarity as a source of moralizing and humanizing 'social power' and called for social revolution to destroy the institutions responsible for disabling this power. SolFed similarly argue that solidarity is a means of overcoming powerlessness, in other words, of empowering workers. On the primitivist side of the debate, the Unabomber Manifesto positively celebrates power. 'Human beings have a need ... for something that we will call the "power process"'. This process is not the same as a lust for power – which might be linked to state domination – and it does not exist in all people to the same degree. Nevertheless the power process is about 'goal, effort ... attainment of goal' and 'autonomy' and it is properly satisfied when individuals have the opportunity to fulfil meaningful, moderately difficult 'drives'. This kind of power is usually denied in civilization but can be realized through engagement with civilization's destruction. Perlman, who finds revolution in remembrance, similarly defines the state's abolition with reference to power. The memory of the past, of the time before Leviathan, is 'a power ... a power to remove [man's] Leviathanic mask while still enmeshed in a Leviathanic web'.[64]

Anarchists influenced by postmodern and poststructuralist thought adopt a similarly open approach to power. However, rather than seeing power as something to be claimed by workers from the state or as an essential human drive, they conceptualize power within the context of the rhizome. Here, power might be arranged hierarchically and it might be concentrated at particular sites. Yet power is transgressive and transformative. As Todd May explains, it can be 'suppressive' or 'productive', it 'suppresses actions, events, and people, but creates them as well'.[65] Power is neither to be abolished nor possessed. To think of power in these conflictual ('binary') terms is to misunderstand it. Power must be utilized in new and different ways, not relocated.

The three alternatives are mapped below:

Three Anarchist Views of Power

	State critique	Means of struggle	Legitimate power
Anarcho-syndicalism/communism	Exploitative	Foster solidarity	Collective/class
Primitivists	Alienating	Mass rebellion/ self-assertion/ regeneration	Individual/mass
Postmoderns	Hierarchical	Networking	Local, diverse, non-hierarchical

Anarchists often argue that their critique of power is a distinctive mark of their ideology and they regularly compare their understandings to competing Marxist ideas. Yet it does not follow from their denunciation of state power that they reject the use of power in support of anarchist change and/or the development of anarchy. The significant division between anarchists on the issue of power is where it should be located. Power is not to be despised, whatever anarchists claim to the contrary.

anarchism and liberty

Anarchist theories of government, power and authority suggest that the state is an unnecessary evil. There are good reasons to seek its abolition and, contrary to the fears and suspicions of the state's supporters, there is no reason to link its disappearance to savagery and disorder. On the contrary, the abolition of the state will put an end to violence and repression and herald a new – more harmonious – social order. Moreover, it will release individuals from the constraints of authority and enable them to enjoy their freedom.

It is possible to extrapolate three anarchist conceptions of freedom from the critiques of authority. For example, the critique of command supports an idea of liberty as autonomy: the condition in which individuals determine their own affairs and subject their decisions to conscience or reason. The critique of control supports a concept of individuality: the liberty individuals enjoy to explore their creative potential and to develop their particular talents and capabilities. Finally, the critique of corruption supports a notion of altruism or brotherhood, in which individuals are able to fulfil their social roles and relationships through association with others. Anarchists combine these conceptions of authority and liberty in different ways. For example, Tolstoy linked his critique of authority as a form of moral corruption to an idea of freedom as autonomy. The only true liberty, he argued 'consists in every man being able to live and act according to his own judgement'.[66] Similarly, Kropotkin tied his critique of authority as dependence to an altruistic conception of liberty inspired by the idea – which he called the principle of mutual aid – that individual freedom is inextricably linked to the freedom of the whole.

Moreover, anarchists tend to regard these different conceptions of liberty as interconnected ideas, not discrete categories of thought.

For example, Malatesta argued that anarchists supported communism because they believed it to be 'the realisation of brotherhood,
and the best guarantee for individual freedom'.[67] Likewise,
Kropotkin argued that the solidarity that characterized altruism
supported both private judgement and individuality. In his extended
essay, *Modern Science and Anarchism*, he argued:

> Free play for the individual, for the full development of his individ-
> ual gifts – *for his individualization*. In other words, no actions are
> *imposed* upon the individual by a fear or punishment; none is
> required from him by society, but those which receive his free
> acceptance. *In a society of equals* this would be quite sufficient for
> preventing those unsociable actions that might be harmful to other
> individuals and to society itself, and for favoring the steady moral
> growth of that society.[68]

In the 1970s the Kropotkinite Roel Van Duyn also drew altruism
together with individuality, though his project was to show that
individuality should support altruism. The 'marriage between
aggression and co-operation, between receptiveness and activity,
between creativity and love can provide us with a way forward, a way
towards the true freedom which is nothing less than every man's
creative participation in universal solidarity and love'.[69]

In a recent polemic, Murray Bookchin has argued that anarchist
contestations of liberty reflect a deep philosophical division in the
movement. He traces the roots of this division to two incompatible
views of the individual. The first, 'focuses overwhelmingly on the
abstract individual ... supports personal autonomy, and ... celebrates the notion of *liberty from* [constraint]'. The second is an
'ethical' idea, encapsulated in the notion of '*freedom for*'. It 'seeks to
create a free society, in which humanity as a whole – and hence the
individual as well – enjoys the advantages of free political and economic institutions'. Bookchin calls the first 'lifestyle' anarchism,
because he thinks that its advocates believe 'that liberty and autonomy can be achieved by making changes in personal sensibilities and
lifeways, giving less attention to changing material and cultural conditions'. He calls the second 'social anarchism'. His terminology is
confusing, not least anarchists associated with the journal *Social
Anarchism* define themselves by a commitment to a 'political philosophy and personal lifestyle'.[70] Nevertheless, identifying himself with
the social anarchist position Bookchin argues that social anarchists

respect 'the importance of gaining individual freedom and personal autonomy' but that they believe that 'the truly free individual is at once an active agent in and the embodiment of a truly free society'.

The argument has been fleshed out in a debate between L. Susan Brown (put by Bookchin in the lifestyle corner) and the social anarchist Janet Biehl. Brown defines liberty as private judgement and individuality, sometimes running these ideas together. Anarchism, she argues, 'asserts that human individuals are best suited to decide for themselves how to run the affairs of their own lives' and affirms 'the individual's freedom to use and develop his or her capacities'. She calls her idea 'existential individualism' on the grounds that an idea of 'becoming' is superior – and more useful to anarchists – than the more straightforwardly liberal conception of freedom as the absence of constraint. However, *pace* Bookchin, she argues that existential individualism leads neither to introspection nor to an egotistic regard for the self. It supports a strong notion of voluntary co-operation. Indeed, existential individualism is compatible with social anarchism: it provides an impetus for voluntary association and, in communism, a basis for individuality.[71]

Biehl's critique suggests that this last assertion is mistaken and she traces the roots of Brown's error to her treatment of the individual as an abstract entity, divorced from its social background. Because Brown considers the individual as a self-determining entity, Biehl argues, she wrongly posits association on a notion of 'choice'. Whilst it's possible that autonomous individuals might decide to associate, Biehl believes that the priority Brown attaches to the individual makes the choice of communism an unlikely one. Moreover, because the individuals Brown describes are 'constitutionally unable to recognise a basic connectedness with one another' the quality of any resulting association will be significantly impaired.[72]

In a review of the Brown-Biehl debate, Thomas Martin argues that the differences between anarchists on the question of liberty are not philosophical. Whilst Bookchin is right to highlight the difficulty of imagining a situation in which individuals might choose lifestyles free from external influences, he is wrong to suggest that Brown's concern – to defend the individual's freedom to determine how to live her life – requires her to treat individuals in this abstract manner. However, he admits that the issue between 'lifestyle' and 'social' anarchists revolves around the different and 'incommensurable' ways in which they understand the relationship between the individual and the community. In other words 'social' and 'lifestyle' anarchists have different sociological theories about the ways in which free individuals enter into social relationships. Bookchin's 'social' view is strongly communitarian, Brown's 'lifestyle' conception, libertarian.[73]

The communitarian view, supported by Biehl and Bookchin, is that individuals are legitimately shaped by the moral, social and cultural mores of their communities. In Bookchin's view 'the making of that "whole" we call a rounded, creative, and richly variegated human being crucially depends upon community supports'. Individual socialization does not inhibit individuals from leading autonomous lives. To the contrary, it provides them with the wherewithal to exercise their freedom. Without community, 'there would be no real self to distort – only a fragmented, wriggling, frail, and pathological thing'. His pithy conclusion is that 'the making of a human being ... is a collective process'.[74] For libertarian or 'lifestyle' critics like Brown, Bookchin's collective processes threaten to cut down the individual's realm of free decision-making and are sources of potential oppression.

The sociological differences between anarchist communitarians and libertarians do not necessarily inhibit political agreement. To give an illustration, there is a long tradition in anarchist thought which defines individuality in terms of sexuality. The general insight is that 'sex undermines Authority'. More precisely, as Alex Comfort argued, 'anti-sexualism of authoritarian societies' springs from 'the vague perception that freedom here might lead to a liking for freedom elsewhere'; and that '[p]eople who have eroticised their experience of themselves ... are ... inconveniently unwarlike'.[75] This tradition of anti-authoritarianism has a number of dimensions, but is strongly associated with feminism. In this context, 'lifestyle' and 'social' anarchists have been able to develop a common politics. For example, Emma Goldman's view (which was founded on the broadly existentialist idea that woman's emancipation depended on 'her inner regeneration' and her ability 'to cut loose from the weight of prejudices, traditions, and customs') was that anarchy would liberate women from the subordinate social role associated with marriage and enable them to find fulfilment in heterosexual, family relationships. From a starting point that is closer to 'social' anarchism, the Anarcha-feminist International arrives at a similar conclusion. Liberation requires that the 'traditional patriarchal nuclear family should be replaced by free associations between men and women based on equal right to decide for both parts and with respect for the individual person's autonomy and integrity'.[76]

Where anarchists have had political disagreements it is often because they dispute the sources of domination or oppression in the state, not because they have different ideas about what constitutes 'woman' (though this is an important debate in other feminist circles). Anarcha-feminists like Nicki Clarke link liberation to overcoming the alienation exhibited in and through the pornographic objectification of women in commodity culture. Anarchists associated with *Class War* divorce 'middle class' feminist concerns with pornography from the power relations that support capitalist forms of exploitation: the problem is not the 'pictures of naked adults having sex' it is the 'damaging, hierarchical and sexist class society that introduces the idea of sexual abuse and male power and dominance over women'.[77]

The debate between communitarians and libertarians adds an important dimension to anarchist discussions of the state and the organization of anarchy but it does not suggest any particular mapping between state critiques and anarchist ideals. It is possible to argue – as Guérin did – that the collective struggle against exploitation will support libertarian ends or, as Tolstoy held, that life in community – Christian fellowship – is based on the exercise of individual conscience. The possible mappings are represented in the diagram below:

Mapping Collectivism, Individualism, Communitarianism and Libertarianism

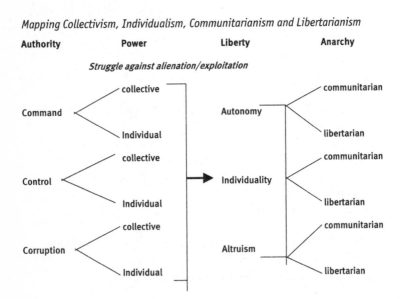

summary

This chapter has examined some leading conceptions of government, authority, power and liberty. There are three key findings:

1. Anarchists reject the state because they believe it to be iniquitous and unnecessary; because it inhibits the expression of freedom, most importantly, through exploitation and alienation.
2. Anarchists typically reject all forms of government, authority and power but accept the possibility of self-government, acknowledge the role of natural authority and rely on notions of collective or individual power to accomplish the state's abolition.
3. Anarchists typically identify anarchism with liberty, but have different ideas about what it means to be free and are divided about whether communitarianism or libertarianism offers the best conditions for the realization of liberty.

further reading

Michael Bakunin, *God and the State*, http://dwardmac.pitzer.edu/Anarchist_Archives

George Crowder, *Classical Anarchism: The Political Thought of Godwin, Proudhon, Bakunin and Kropotkin* (Oxford: Clarendon Press, 1991)

Guy Debord, *The Society of the Spectacle*, http://www.spunk.org.texts/writers.debord/sp000547.txt

Peter Kropotkin, *The State: Its Historic Role*, http://dwardmac.pitzer.edu/Anarchist_Archives

John Marks, *Gilles Deleuze: Vitalism and Multiplicity* (London: Pluto Press, 1998)

Todd May, *The Political Philosophy of Poststructuralist Anarchism* (Pennsylvania: Pennsylvania State University Press, 1994)

Jon Purkis and James Bowen (eds), *Twenty-First Century Anarchism* (London: Cassell, 1997)

William Reichert, 'Anarchism, Freedom and Power', *Ethics*, 79 (2), 1969: 139–49

William Reichert, 'Towards a New Understanding of Anarchism', *Western Political Quarterly*, 20, 1967: 856–65

Alan Ritter, 'The Anarchist Justification of Authority' in

J.R. Pennock and J.W. Chapman (eds), *Nomos XIX: Anarchism*
(New York: New York University Press, 1978)
Dimitrios Roussopoulos (ed.), *The Anarchist Papers* (Montreal:
Black Rose, 1989)

links

Anarcha-feminism (index): http://www.spunk.org/texts/
anarcfem/index.html
Black Flag (anarcho-syndicalist and communist ideas):
http://flag.blackened.net/blackflag
John Moore: http://lemming.mahost.org/johnmoore
Institute for Social Ecology (Murray Bookchin):
http://www.social-ecology.org
The Zabalaza Site (Anarchist, revolutionary syndicalist and anti-
authoritarian movements in South Africa, Lesotho and
Swaziland): http://www.zabalaza.net/archive.htm

notes

1. E. Malatesta, *Anarchy* (London: Freedom Press, 1974), 11.
2. S. Faure, in G. Woodcock, *The Anarchist Reader* (Harmondsworth:
   Penguin, 1983), 62.
3. G. Woodcock, 'Not Any Power' in C. Ward (ed.), *A Decade of Anarchy*
   (London: Freedom Press, 1987), 77.
4. J. Moore, 'Anarchism and Poststructuralism', *Anarchist Studies*, 5 (2),
   1977: 160.
5. E. Goldman, *Red Emma Speaks*, ed. A.K. Shulman (London: Wildwood
   House, 1972), 90–3.
6. M. Rothbard, 'The Anatomy of the State', in *Egalitarianism as a Revolt
   Against Nature and Other Essays*, http://www.mises.org/easaran/
   chap3.asp
7. *The State is Your Enemy* (London: Freedom Press, 1991),
   202; 261.
8. Brian S. 'Reporting from the Frontline', *On Fire* (London: One Off
   Press, 2001), 21.
9. P.H. Douglas, 'Proletarian Political Theory', in C.E. Merriam and H.E.
   Barnes, *A History of Political Theories* (New York: Macmillan, 1932),
   214.

10. L. Tolstoy, *Government is Violence: Essays on Anarchism and Pacifism*, D. Stephens (ed.) (London: Phoenix Press, 1990), 28.

11. Rothbard, *Anatomy of the State*, http://mises.org/easaran/chap3.asp

12. N. Chomsky, *Power and Terror* (New York: Seven Stories Press, 2003), 49; 73.

13. C. Wilson, *Three Essays on Anarchism*, ed. N. Walter (Orkney: Cienfuegos Press, 1979), 1–2.

14. F. Ruby, *The War on Women*, http://spunk.org/library/anarcfem/sp001095.txt

15. http://www.guerrillagirls.com

16. F. Perlman, *Against His-tory, Against Leviathan!* (Detroit: Black & Red, 1983), 41.

17. P. Kropotkin, in R. Baldwin (ed.), *Kropotkin's Revolutionary Pamphlets* (New York: Dover, 1970), 125–6.

18. P. Kropotkin, *Wars and Capitalism* (London: Freedom Press, 1915), 1.

19. Anarchist Communist Federation, *As We See It* (London: ACF, n.d.), 5.

20. K. Goaman, 'Globalisation Versus Humanisation: Contemporary Anti-Capitalism and Anarchism', *Anarchist Studies*, 11 (2), 2003.

21. N. Walter, *About Anarchism* (London: Freedom Press, 2002), 34.

22. 'What is globalization?' from *Do or Die, Voices of Ecological Resistance*, 8, http://rts/gn/apc/org/glob/htm

23. M. Bakunin, in K.J. Kenafick, *Marxism, Freedom and the State*, http://flag.blackened.net/daver/anarchism/bakunin/marxnfree.html

24. R.P. Wolff, *In Defence of Anarchism* (New York: Harper & Row, 1970), 9–14.

25. A. Rand, 'What is Capitalism?', *Capitalism: The Unknown Ideal* (New York: Signet, 1967), 17.

26. P. Kropotkin, *Act For Yourselves* (London: Freedom Press, 1988), 82.

27. D. Marsden, *The New Freewoman*, 1913, http://www.nonserviam.com/egoistarchive/marsden

28. H. Read, *The Philosophy of Anarchism* (London: Freedom Press, 1941), 12.

29. H. Read, *One Man Manifesto*, D. Goodway (ed.), (London: Freedom Press, 1994), 201.

30. J. Zerzan, *Running on Emptiness* (Los Angeles: Feral House, 2002), 6; 16; 159.

31. N. Clarke, *RAW*, http://www.spunk.org/texts/anarcfem/sp000887.txt

32. A. Bonanno, *Armed Joy*, 1977, http://www.geocities.com/kk_abacus/ioaa/a_joy.html

33. Anon, 'Superb!' *Poll Tax Riot* (London: Acab Press, 1990), 49.

34. L. Tolstoy, *The Kingdom of God and Peace Essays* (London: Humphrey Milford, 1936), 343; 389–403.
35. J. McQuinn, *What is Ideology?* http://primitivism.com/ideology.htm
36. Perlman, *Against His-tory*, 38.
37. P.-J. Proudhon, *General Idea of the Revolution in the Nineteenth Century* (London: Pluto Press, 1989), 294.
38. L. Tolstoy, *Government is Violence*, 98–9.
39. Kropotkin, *Revolutionary Pamphlets*, 200–05.
40. R. Rocker, *Nationalism and Culture* (St Paul, Minnesota: Croixside Press, 1978), 243.
41. F. Perlman, 'The Continuing Appeal of Nationalism', *Anarchy: A Journal of Desire Armed*, 37 (Summer 1993), http://www.spunk.org/ library/pubs/ajoda/37/sp000787.txt
42. Zerzan, *Running on Emptiness*, 76.
43. B. Black, 'The Abolition of Work', in H. Ehrlich (ed.) *Reinventing Anarchy, Again* (Edinburgh: AK Press, 1996), 238–9.
44. M. Hern, 'The Promise of Deschooling', *Social Anarchism*, 25, 1988, http://library.nothingness.org/articles/SA/en/display/130
45. P. Kropotkin, *Words of a Rebel* (Montreal: Black Rose, 1992), 62.
46. Anarchist Communist Federation, *As We See It* (London: ACF, n.d.), 4.
47. SolFed, *An Introduction to Solidarity Federation* (Manchester: SolFed, 1988), 3–4.
48. F. Perlman, *The Reproduction of Daily Life*, 1969, http://www.spunk.org/ library/writers.perlman/sp001702/repro.html
49. Zerzan, *Running on Emptiness*, 80.
50. T. Kaczynski, *The Unabomber Manifesto*, http://www.thecourier.com/ manifest.htm
51. M. Albert, 'Anarchists', in E. Bircham and J. Charlton (eds), *Anti-Capitalism: A Guide to the Movement* (London: Bookmark Publications, 2001), 324.
52. P. Kropotkin, *The State: Its Historic Role* (London: Freedom Press, 1943), 10.
53. E. Malatesta, *Anarchy* (London: Freedom Press, 1974), 13.
54. J. McEwan, 'Anarchism and the Cybernetics of Self-Organising Systems' in C. Ward (ed.), *A Decade of Anarchy*, 57.
55. J. Westall, 'On Authority', in C. Ward (ed.), *A Decade of Anarchy*, 40.
56. M. Bakunin, *God and the State* (London: London Anarchist Groups, 1893), 18–19.
57. H. Read, *The Philosophy of Anarchism* (London: Freedom Press, 1941), 15.
58. Perlman, *Against His-tory*, 57.

59. Proudhon, *General Idea of the Revolution*, 295.

60. Kropotkin, *Revolutionary Pamphlets*, 189.

61. R. Rocker, *Anarcho-Syndicalism* (London: Phoenix Press, n.d.), 55.

62. Moore, 'Anarchism and Poststructuralism', 161.

63. J. Moore, 'Maximalist Anarchism/Anarchist Maximalism', *Social Anarchism* 25, 1998, http://library.nothingness.org/articles/SA/en/display/134

64. Perlman, *Against His-tory*, 50.

65. T. May, *The Political Philosophy of Poststructuralist Anarchism* (Pennsylvania: Pennsylvania State University, 1994), 63.

66. L. Tolstoy, *Government is Violence*, D. Stephens (ed.) (London: Phoenix Press, 1990), 58.

67. E. Malatesta, *Life and Ideas*, V. Richards (ed.) (London: Freedom Press, 1977), 31.

68. Kropotkin, *Revolutionary Pamphlets*, 157.

69. R. Van Duyn, *Message of a Wise Kabouter* (London: Duckworth & Co., 1972), 83.

70. M. Bookchin, *Wither Anarchism? A Reply to Recent Anarchist Critics*, 1998, http://www.socialanarchism.org

71. L.S. Brown, 'A Reply to Murray Bookchin's Social Anarchism or Lifestyle Anarchism', *Anarchist Studies*, 4 (2), 1996: 135.

72. J. Biehl, 'A Reply to Susan Brown', *Anarchist Studies*, 4 (2), 1996: 143–7.

73. T. Martin, 'Bookchin, Biehl, Brown', *Anarchist Studies*, 6 (1), 1998: 43.

74. M. Bookchin, *The Modern Crisis* (Philadelphia: New Society Publishers, 1986), 35.

75. A. Comfort, *Writings Against Power and Death*, ed. D. Goodway (London: Freedom Press, 1994), 25.

76. *Bulletin of the Anarchist International*, http://www.powertech.no/anarchy/ai/html

77. *Class War*, 'Let's Talk About Sex', http://www.spunk.org/library/sex/sp001711.html

anarchy

We have always lived in slums and holes in the wall. We will know how to accommodate ourselves for a time. For you must not forget that we can also build. It is we who built these palaces and cities, here in Spain and in America and everywhere. We, the workers. We can build others to take their place. And better ones. We are not in the least afraid of ruins. We are going to inherit the earth. There is not the slightest doubt about that. The bourgeoisie might blast and ruin its own world before it leaves the stage of history. We carry a new world, here, in out hearts, and that world is growing in this minute.

(Buenaventura Durruti in *The People Armed*, p. 229)

Utopian? Guilty Your Honour
Revolutionaries are often reproached for being utopian, of being dreamers. Yes, we are dreamers, because like children, we don't like nightmares. Yes, we are utopian. This utopia is not a heavenly paradise come to Earth. Neither is it a return to a mythical Golden Age. This 'other' place is a symbolic territory, based on our revolutionary refusal to put up with a world founded on the violence of class and ethnic or sexual domination, of the exploitation of labour and the body, of alienation.

(Anarchist Federation, 'Beyond Resistance', p. 14)

Anarchists are habitually accused of being utopians and of dreaming of impossible futures. In discussions of anarchy, anarchists have usually tried to debunk this as myth, but have at the same time held fast to visions of radical social transformation. This chapter reviews some anarchist ideas of anarchy through three frameworks of analysis. It begins with a discussion of anarchist anthropology, reviewing the very different conclusions anarchists have drawn from the study of pre-state or preliterate, 'primitive' societies. The second section of the chapter looks at the relationship between anarchism and utopianism, presenting an anarcho-syndicalist and an eco-anarchist model of organization. The final section considers the ways in which anarchists have attempted to put their principles into practice, looking again at anarcho-syndicalism and, developing the discussion of liberty, the idea of anarchist community.

anarchy and anthropology

In 1963 in the British journal *Anarchy*, Kenneth Maddock argued that anarchists who drew on anthropological studies of primitive or stateless societies were purveyors of social myths. Their concern was not so much to show how primitive societies functioned, but to show 'what the future would be'. Their analyses were 'reverse reflections, critiques, of the present' which built into the past 'precisely those qualities lacking in the present'. And their aim was to spur 'men on to action'.[1] Undoubtedly Maddock was right to suggest that anarchist studies of stateless societies were broadly posited on a critique of the state. But his suggestion that anarchists have habitually treated stateless societies as models of anarchy wrongly suggests that they have viewed the relationship between statelessness and anarchy in a uniform way. Contrary to Maddock, it is possible to distinguish four schools of thought. Kropotkin is a representative of the first school, though he was torn between two views. On the one hand, he represented statelessness as a primitive condition through which humanity had evolved and, on the other, he argued that traditional or 'primitive' ways of life were examples of statelessness that should be protected. Harold Barclay is a representative of the second approach. Barclay argues that stateless societies are functioning anarchies and uses anthropological evidence to examine the conditions of anarchy's operation. Murray Bookchin is the leading theorist of the third school. Bookchin's view is that the anthropological studies of preliterate peoples provide an insight into the ecological system and an ethical guide to the proper organization of anarchy. Zerzan and Perlman are representative of the final school. These writers – particularly Zerzan – review anthropological arguments about statelessness in order to uncover the behaviours and attitudes that have been lost to the destructive power of civilization. These four approaches point to broad agreement about the status of anarchy in relation to the state, but reveal very different approaches to questions of organization.

Kropotkin's interest in anthropology and the study of stateless societies was captured in his book, *Mutual Aid*.[2] In this work, Kropotkin set out to counter the idea, associated with Social Darwinism, that nature was 'red in tooth and claw' – that individuals were necessarily locked into a competitive struggle for existence in which only the fittest would survive. Kropotkin met this argument with the contention that struggle was a collective endeavour in which the most co-operative would flourish. He further suggested that the degree to which individuals would co-operate was deter- mined by environmental factors. Kropotkin's analysis of these factors was quite complex, but his general hypothesis was that the state inhibited co-operation and that anarchy encouraged it. In order to test this theory, Kropotkin turned to 'primitive' or pre-state societies to show how the principle of mutual aid had evolved.

Kropotkin drew on a range of anthropological evidence to show how 'primitive' peoples practised mutual aid. Following Victorian conventions he classified these peoples as 'savages' and 'barbarians'. These classifications did not imply a simple judgement about the superiority of modern life over either 'savagery' or 'barbarism'. Indeed, Kropotkin believed that the moral principles of these primi- tive peoples were in many ways superior to those of the moderns. For example, whereas modern society was distinguished by violence, primitive society was characterized by natural solidarity: 'hospitality ... respect for human life, the sense of reciprocal obligation, compas- sion for the weak, courage, extending even to the sacrifice of the self for others ...'. Nonetheless, Kropotkin tended to treat these forms of social life as outmoded. This judgement in part reflected his awareness that very few of these societies had practised communism, his eco- nomic ideal. In the other part, it was informed by his view that 'savage' and 'barbarian' peoples adopted social practices that did not sit easily with Victorian social mores. Kropotkin was eager to provide rational explanations for these practices. But his explanations suggested that primitive forms of behaviour had been exploded by subsequent social and moral developments. For example, Kropotkin argued:

> Primitive man may have thought it very right ... to eat his aged
> parent when they became a charge upon the community ... He may
> have also thought it useful to the community to kill his new-born
> children, and only keep two or three in each family ...

In our days ideas have changed, but the means of subsistence are no longer what they were in the Stone Age. Civilized man is not in the position of the savage family who have to choose between two evils: either to eat the aged parents or else all to get insufficient nourishment ...[3]

When Kropotkin found examples of statelessness in the body of the state, he took a different position. Here he drew on a romantic view of the peasantry inherited from his pre-anarchist association with the Russian populist movement. He was also inspired by his exploratory work in Eastern Siberia, and the intimate knowledge he had gained as a geographer of the peoples who inhabited this remote region. Kropotkin's experiences helped to convince him that the organization of village life could serve as the nucleus for post-revolutionary organization and that the peasant commune should be preserved as the basic unit of anarchy. Moreover it strengthened his regard for traditional and indigenous ways of life. Indeed, though his analysis of social evolution suggested that the loss of barbarism was a sign of progress, he was persuaded that modern primitive societies were prototype anarchies. For example, he regarded the Doukhobors, a religious sect of Siberian peasant exiles, 'natural anarchists'. Driven by his admiration for their rejection of Tsarist authority and their anti-militarism, he worked with Tolstoy to ease their flight from persecution in Russia and to secure for them a new home in Canada.

Harold Barclay recasts the relationship between anarchy, state-lessness and anthropology. Stepping back from the developmental approach suggested by Kropotkin, he argues that the trend towards the state 'should not be interpreted as an evolutionary scheme in which cultural history is a one-way street where all "tribal" societies must become state type societies'. Moreover, whereas Kropotkin turned to anthropology to distinguish states from pre-state societies, Barclay classifies stateless societies on a continuum that stretches from anarchy to archy. At one end of the scale, anarchy emphasizes 'voluntary co-operation'. At the other, archy is characterized by 'the prevalence of legal sanctions'. Primitive or stateless societies veer towards anarchy but fall into the middle ground, an area consisting of 'marginal forms of anarchy' or rudimentary governments. Whilst Barclay criticizes modern anthropologists for failing to treat stateless societies as functioning anarchies, he does not believe that their existence indicates that the abandonment of the state is politically or culturally feasible. To the contrary, anthropology suggests that state-lessness is only sustainable in certain conditions. Barclay outlines the possibilities by pinpointing the factors that explain 'the descent into the state'. The two most important are the emergence of hierarchy and the 'ideology of superiority/inferiority'. These stimulate a further six socio-economic factors: 'population, sedentarism, agriculture, a complex division of labour, a redistribution system and private property'. Anarchic ways of life are possible only where these factors do not arise and/or where they are unimportant in social life. In Barclay's view, the relevant conditions are 'most likely to be found in the acephalous societies of pre-colonial Africa'.[4]

Murray Bookchin's work revives some of Kropotkin's themes. John Clark places him in a tradition that extends to Reclus rather than Kropotkin, but his relationship to the latter is, nonetheless, strong. Indeed, Bookchin develops Kropotkin's rejection of Social Darwinism and his characterization of nature – in his terms, the ecosystem – by the principle of mutual aid. Like Kropotkin, he associates the ecosystem with ethics. In particular, Bookchin argues that the ecosystem demonstrates the absurdity and meaninglessness of hierarchy and that it operates on a principle of 'unity in diversity'. Defining this latter principle, Bookchin argues: 'the more differentiated the life-form and the environment in which it exists the more acute is its overall sensorium, the greater its flexibility, and the more active its participation in its own environment'.[5]

The important difference between Kropotkin and Bookchin is that whilst Kropotkin suggested that nature was the foundation for ethics, in Bookchin's view, it provides only a 'matrix for an ethics'. The redefinition of terms is reflected in Bookchin's attitude toward progress and in his treatment of stateless societies. On the first point, Bookchin rejects Kropotkin's idea that changes in social life can be mapped onto an evolutionary schema of progressive moral development. Indeed, he castigates Kropotkin for adopting an overly optimistic view of progress, even categorizing him as a 'technological determinist'. On the second point, when Bookchin, very much in the spirit of Kropotkin, draws back to the study of preliterate peoples, he is not so much interested in studying patterns of human behaviour as he is in highlighting the relationships which preliterate peoples establish with their environment. For example, in the *Ecology of Freedom* Bookchin finds that preliterate peoples do not respect age hierarchies that treat children as lesser personalities than adults, or indeed any hierarchy which gives individuals in the community permanent advantages in property, leadership or exchange. Bookchin applauds this aspect of 'primitive' life, but he regards it as a consequence of a deeper set of values embedded in preliterate societies – their organic relationship to the eco-system and their inability or unwillingness to distinguish between human and non-human worlds. Bookchin admits that in the 1960s and '70s he had 'an excessive enthusiasm for certain aspects of aboriginal and organic societies'. His mature work, however, concentrates on the ways in which this ethical matrix might be recovered, not on preserving the behaviours and habits of the preliterate peoples it supports. Bookchin's call is to

> ... [r]ecover the continuum between our 'first nature' and our 'second nature,' our natural world and our social world, our biological being and our rationality. Latent within us are ancestral memories that only an ecological society and sensibility can 'resurrect.' The history of human reason has not yet reached its culmination, much less its end. Once we can 'resurrect' our subjectivity and restore it to its heights of sensibility, then in all likelihood that history will have just begun.[6]

Perlman and Zerzan define primitive society in opposition to civilization. They take a developmental view of the relationship between the two. However, they invert the indicators of development suggested by Kropotkin's evolutionary system to define changes in the behaviours of primitive peoples in terms of the corrupting influence of domestication rather than the progressive march of civilization. Perlman located these changes in the shift from nomadic ways of life and the emergence of tools as 'productive forces'. Zerzan's view is that 'the wrong turn for humanity was the Agricultural Revolution'. This brought 'a rise in labor, a decrease in sharing, an increase in violence, a shortening of lifespan' and alienation 'from each other, from the natural world, from their bodies'.[7]

Like Kropotkin and Bookchin, Zerzan draws on mainstream anthropology to support this view, but he uses these studies to describe what the absence of civilization means, rather than to abstract an anarchist ethic from the stateless condition. The contrast he draws between primitivism and civilization is stark. Without exception, Zerzan argues, the peoples in 'non-agricultural' society 'knew no organized violence'. Elsewhere he argues: the 'violence of primitives – human sacrifice, cannibalism, head-hunting, slavery, etc. – ... was not ended by culture, but in fact commenced with it'. His response to anthropologists who cite the slavery and hierarchy of Northwest Coast Indians as evidence of such violence, is that these fishing people had begun to domesticate nature, taming dogs and growing tobacco as a minor crop.[8]

One of Zerzan's concerns is to outline the ways in which primitive peoples relate to their world and to highlight the benefits they derive from this relationship. For example, he suggests that non-agricultural peoples have a much greater sensory awareness than their domesticated counterparts. Bushmen can 'see four moons of Jupiter with the unaided eye and hear a single engine light plane seventy miles away'. Typically, they rely on their senses – particularly of smell and touch – to interpret the world. In contrast to agricultural peoples, they communicate visually and by sharing experiences. They do not rely on language alone. Zerzan suggests that these skills of perception and communication are reflected in a positive attitude towards time and work. For example, he notes with approval how the Mbuti of southern Africa have little interest in linear time. They believe that 'by a correct fulfilment of the present, the past and future will take care of themselves'. His more general point is that life in primitive society is 'in fact largely one of leisure, intimacy with nature, sensual wisdom, sexual equality, and health'. Denying the charge that this image is 'Rousseauvian [sic] noble savage nonsense', Zerzan reviews recent academic findings and comments:

> Prehistory is now characterized more by intelligence, egalitarianism and sharing, leisure time, a great degree of sexual equality, robusticity and health, with no evidence at all of organized violence ... We're still living, of course, with the cartoonish images, the caveman pulling the woman into the cave, Neanderthal meaning somebody who is a complete brute and subhuman, and so on. But the real picture has been wholly revised.[9]

Perlman paints a similar picture, though he relies far less than Zerzan on modern anthropology to support his view. At one point, however, he turns to a discussion of the !Kung, who 'miraculously survived as a community of free human beings into our own exterminating age', to estimate the quality of primitive life. The !Kung, he notes, 'cultivated nothing except themselves'. They spent their time feasting and celebrating and 'played full-time, except when they slept' and derived 'deep inner joy' from their life in common. Like

Zerzan, Perlman is keen to contest the view that primitivism describes a rude or meagre way of life. People in primitive, pre-Leviathanic societies were inventive; they had tools and they devised ways of satisfying their needs and wants. Many 'kingless people' Perlman argues, 'rode horses and some wielded iron implements'. They engaged positively with their environment and they lived well. Pressing his point, Perlman contrasts the life of the Possessed – nomads who wandered all over the earth, from Eurasia to America – with the modern Dispossessed. The former 'were very fond of animals; they knew the animals as cousins'. He continues: '[s]ome of the women learned from birds and winds to scatter seeds. Some of the men learned from wolves and eagles to hunt'. But they did not work. For the most part, the women performed dances and 'abandoned themselves to visions, myths and ceremonies'. Yet life was not a struggle since the wanderers 'loved nature and nature reciprocated their love'. Indeed, wherever people went 'they found affluence'. In contrast to the Dispossessed who live in 'abundance', the Possessed did not 'go to the theatre and see plays ... sprawl in front of the TV and consume the entire worldwide spectacle'. Nor did they possess very much – 'houses and garages, cars and stereo equipment'. But their life, unlike that of the Dispossessed, was one of richness and not lived 'in the pits and on the margins of industrialization'.[10]

These different analyses of primitive or stateless society support two broad conclusions about the status of anarchy. The first is that anarchy is a natural condition. As Barclay argues, it is the most common and 'oldest type of polity which has characterised ... human history'.[11] Anarchy appears unnatural only because history has favoured the organization of the state and because, even in a globalized world where the powers of the state appear to be challenged, this historical trend is unlikely to be reversed. Yet even though the state has endured, the study of stateless societies suggests that it is both impermanent and alien. The second point, which flows from this, is that the destruction of anarchy came about through the emergence of a state system. Studies of statelessness do not suggest that the state developed with the same rapidity in all parts of the globe. Kropotkin suggested that the state was a European invention that was exported to the rest of the world through colonization. Barclay offers a similar explanation. The state was developed as a prototype 'in only a few places'. In most instances, 'it was copied from the original ... invariably under duress'. But once the state was instituted the process of

replication was assured.[12] Perlman puts a similar case. The birth of
Leviathan set in motion a fundamental change in organization.
Although the beast was resisted and although for many years people
found ways of escaping or withdrawing from it, in time, it extended
its octopus-like tentacles to all parts of the globe. And as smaller
Leviathans were swallowed by larger ones the routes of possible
escape were eventually closed off.

This unusual consensus breaks down when anarchists evaluate
primitive or stateless societies as models for anarchy. Discussions
about the potential for modelling anarchy in this way have focused
on two issues: the possibility of reconciling traditional or primitive
ways of life with anarchist values, and the possibility of recovering
primitive modes of behaviour in technologically developed societies.

The first issue, which has rumbled on more or less uninterrupted
since the publication of Kropotkin's *Mutual Aid*, is about the space
traditional societies provide for creativity and self-expression. In
contrast to Barclay, some anarchists have treated traditional stateless
societies as straightforward indicators of anarchy, suggesting that
there is no conflict between membership of the community and
individuality. Notwithstanding his suspicion of social myths,
Maddock claimed that the African tribe, the Nuer, 'if not actually
living in anarchy ... were as close to it as social existence could be'.
Such Kropotkinite appreciations of indigenous ways of life chime in
with the efforts of non-European anarchists to develop principles of
organization designed to protect cultural traditions. For example,
Teanau Tuiono defines the Maori struggle for self-determination –
Tino Rangatiratanga – as a battle against capitalism and colonialism
that is directed towards a 'vision of society free of racism, class
exploitation, women's oppression, homo-phobia and the oppression
of indigenous peoples'. Yet neither the struggle nor the vision
conforms to European standards. Indeed, there are 'some aspects of
Tino Rangatiratanga ... that are for Maori only'. In conclusion
Tuiono argues:

> It is simply dangerous to assume that what happens in Britain or
> Europe can be simply applied to NZ [New Zealand]. Where there
> are broader trends that are the same, we need an indigenous analysis
> of class struggle and capitalism in NZ not the borrowed writings of
> British authors applied mindlessly and indiscriminately to a country
> 12,000 miles away. The Polynesian populace is overwhelmingly
> working class ... our values and outlook are not the same as British

workers. We need to build an indigenous analysis and political strategy that relates to the realities of surviving capitalism in our own little part of the world.[13]

Few anarchists would take issue with this point. Yet, a good number remain to be persuaded that anarchism can always accommodate the practices of primitive or stateless peoples. Rather than taking their lead from Kropotkin's 'cult of the primitive', they turn instead to Bakunin who, for all his enthusiasm for rural insurrection, argued that even when freely organized, traditional societies were unlikely 'miraculously [to] create an ideal organiza- tion, conforming in all respects to our dreams'. For example, the traditions embraced by Russian village life were often oppressively patriarchal. The peasantry, he argued, were 'superstitious, fanatically religious, and controlled by their priests' – especially the women (!).[14] In this spirit, John Pilgrim took issue with Maddock's findings, questioned the norms of stateless groups and argued that the mere absence of state controls did not rule out widespread coercion, the existence of class divisions and rampant materialism. In evidence, he pointed to the habits of the Kwakiutl Indians, arguing that they had 'created a society that, in its economic ethos, showed a greater similarity to the current American ethos of conspicuous consump- tion, than to the type of society that anarchists would like to see'. His conclusion was that statelessness was desirable, but not on the primitive model.[15] George Woodcock took the analysis back to Russia. After a disappointing visit to the Doukhobors in 1963, he complained that their behaviour did not live up to Kropotkin's rosy portrayal. They combined a distrust of Tsarism with a rigid observance of temporal and spiritual authority and a disturbing habit of requesting others to perform acts prohibited by their reli- gion. Woodcock concluded that there was a gulf between the ways of life practised in 'natural' stateless societies and the kind of 'natural' or legitimate authority anarchist critics of the state had in mind when they considered the issue of promising. His report of a conversation with a member of the community about the role of Michael the Archangel was as follows:

'Michael is just our spiritual leader,' Joe explained blandly.
'But he still seems to have a great say in your practical affairs.'
'It depends on what you mean by *say*. He gives no orders. We are free men. We don't obey anybody. But he gives us advice.'
'Do you always accept?'

'If we know what's good for us, we do.'

'Why?'

'Because we know Michael the Archangel is always right.'[16]

The issue of technology has also occupied anarchists for some time, but the emergence of primitivism has altered the terms of anarchist debate. Kropotkin's approach to the issue was to find ways of using technology that would facilitate the expression of mutual aid. The solution he offered in *Fields, Factories and Workshops* was to reorganize production on a local level, integrating agriculture and industry so that each area could produce for its own needs.[17] It required the imaginative application of advanced technology – particularly electric power – and the introduction of intensive farming methods. Bookchin has different priorities – social ecology, not mutual aid. Yet his model of anarchy anticipates a similar restructuring of the economy and the application of technology. In social ecology, production is driven by needs rather than consumer wants. The present impetus 'to mass-produce goods in highly mech-anized installations will be vastly diminished by the communities' overwhelming emphasis on quality and permanence'. But com-munes recycle their organic waste, 'integrate solar, wind, hydraulic, and methane-producing installations'.

Zerzan's and Perlman's solution is to abandon civilization, cul-ture and technology altogether. Though both writers deny that primitivism demands the abolition of tools, both also – particularly Zerzan – tap into the study of stateless societies to highlight the advantages that the abandonment of technology will bring. As John Fliss suggests, primitivist arguments are designed to provide 'a counterweight to technology. Primitivism as a whole is the position of a counter-force to technological progress'.[18] This conclusion marks a radical departure from other forms of anarchist thought. For example, when Tolstoy looked forward to anarchy, he argued that 'culture, useful culture will not be destroyed. It will certainly not be necessary for people to revert to tillage of the land with sticks, or to lighting-up with torches'.[19] More recently, a correspondent to *Black Flag* suggests: the aim of anarcho-syndicalist struggle is to turn technology into 'a universal resource'. Its destruction in the name of anarchy 'would be ... disastrous'. Quoting Bakunin the writer con-cludes, such an act would 'condemn all humanity – which is infin-itely too numerous today to exist ... on the simple gifts of nature ... to ... death by starvation'.[20] Even Thoreau distinguished himself from the primitivists. As Nancy Rosenblum remarks when, in 1845 he famously withdrew to his hut at Walden Pond, Massachusetts, to live a simple, independent life he 'did not prescribe severe self-sufficiency for everyone ... or even for himself once he returned to the city'.[21] It's easy to sympathize with the primitivist critique of civilization and technology, but less easy to see how primitivism might be enjoyed.

Summary of the debate

	Status of anarchy	Characteristics of pre-state	'Primitive' and anarchy	Technology
Kropotkin	Natural	Mutual aid	Structure anarchy to recover ethic	Apply/innovate
Barclay	Natural	Leaderless	Cannot restructure	N/a
Bookchin	Natural	Organic harmony	Structure anarchy to recover ethic	Apply/innovate
Zerzan/ Perlman	Natural	Undomesticated possession	Abandon civilization to recover wild	Abandon

anarchy and utopia

Instead of looking to anthropology to find evidence of anarchy, some anarchists have preferred to investigate the possibilities of anarchist organization through the lens of utopianism. Utopian traditions of theorizing are well established in anarchist thought. However, anarchism has an ambivalent relationship to utopianism. On the one hand, anarchist writers have been anxious to dispel the charge that they are fantasists. On the other, they have attached a high priority to discussions of future organization. In part this ambivalence stems from an attempt to reconcile a desire to show the viability of anarchy with a commitment to experimentation and variety – in other words, from a desire to show that the idea of anarchy is not inconsistent with anarchist principles. In the other part, the ambivalence can be explained by a specific debate with Marxism. In this particular context, the disavowal of utopianism is an attempt to meet the charge, levelled by Marxists, that anarchist thought is 'utopian' in the sense that it is fantastical or impossible. And the affirmation of utopia reflects an eagerness to illustrate the differences between anarchist and Marxist notions of post-revolutionary society and the deficiencies of Marxist an-utopianism. These different positions are outlined below as a prelude to the consideration of two utopian schemes.

The clearest statement of the anarchist suspicion of utopianism appears in Marie Louise Berneri's *Journey Through Utopia*, an analysis of utopian thought from Plato to Huxley. In this book she argued that the outstanding feature of most utopias is their authoritarianism. With notable exceptions like William Morris's *News From Nowhere*, utopias promise material and spiritual satisfaction as well as social and economic equality at the cost of foisting on their ideal citizens a unifying moral ideal. Typically, utopias fail what Berneri called the test of art: Herbert Read's standard of individuality and social experimentation.[22] Some anarchists have taken the critique further, rejecting utopianism in principle. It is not so much the content of utopias that upsets these anarchists but the very idea of perfection – whether it applies to the social order or to the framing of personality. As Rudolf Rocker argues, anarchism 'is no patent solution for all human problems, no Utopia of a perfect social order ... since, on principle, it rejects all absolute schemes and concepts'.[23] A similar view informs a recent critique of Zerzan. Zerzan's treatment of primitive society suggests an 'idealized, hypostatized vision of the past' that is at odds with the critical self-understanding of the social and natural world that informs primitivist critique. It suggests a recommendation for preconceived ideals in a way that constrains free thought.[24]

The suggestion that anarchists should consider what post-revolutionary society might look like does not sit easily with this view. Nonetheless, some anarchists have argued that outlining the operation and benefits of anarchy is a necessary part of securing revolutionary change. Utopias rightly force revolutionaries to consider what they want to achieve and how they might set about realizing their aims. This argument was the basis of Kropotkin's defence of utopianism, for example. Anarchists in this group are sometimes prepared to label their plans as utopias, but they consider their endeavours to be entirely practical. As Bookchin remarks, '[t]he highest realism can be attained only by looking beyond the given state of affairs to a vision of what *should* be, not only what *is*'.[25] Some cast their visions in literary form, on the model of Ursula LeGuin's *The Dispossessed*, though probably more have a 'scientific' feel. Kropotkin's *The Conquest of Bread* (1906), his outline plan for revolutionary action, and *Fields, Factories and Workshops* (1898), his plan for post-revolutionary organization, fit this model.

The specific debate between anarchists and Marxists on the question of utopia turns on a distinction Marx and Engels drew between utopian and scientific socialism. By utopian socialism they referred to the writings of early nineteenth-century socialists – Charles Fourier, Robert Owen and St Simon – whose work was largely devoted to the design of ideal communities. Scientific socialism was the term they gave to their own work. The distinction was not designed to denigrate the work of these early writers, but to suggest that the science of Marxism and, more specifically, the idea of historical development on which it was based, had made any attempt to design ideal futures redundant. It suggested that socialists who refused to accept the 'truth' of Marxist teachings were by definition utopian. Nickolai Bukharin applied this logic in critique of the anarchists. Their refusal to accept Marx's economic theory led anarchists to approach the question of organizing production with a view to supplanting the industrial system rather than enhancing it. This idea was 'utterly utopian'.[26] George Plekhanov advanced a similar case.

> The Anarchists are Utopians. Their point of view has nothing in common with that of modern scientific Socialism. But there are Utopias and Utopians. The great Utopians of the first half of our century were men of genius; they helped forward social science, which in their time was still entirely Utopian. The Utopians of to-day, the Anarchists, are the abstracters of quintessence, who can only fully draw forth some poor conclusions from certain mummified principles.[27]

The anarchist response was two-pronged. Landauer's counter-charge was that the Marxist ideal was too mechanistic. Marxists naively trusted science to 'reveal, calculate and determine the future with certainty from the data and news of the past and the facts and conditions of the present'. But socialism is an art that relies on the rediscovery of spirit. It is utopian because it demands human action. The future – where 'we are going, must go, and must want to go' – can be shaped only by 'deepest conviction and feeling ... of *what ought to be*'. Landauer's plaintive cry was:

> We are poets; and we want to eliminate the scientific swindlers, the Marxists, cold, hollow, spiritless, so that poetic vision, artistically concentrated creativity, enthusiasm, and prophecy will find their

place to act, work and build from now on; in life, with human bodies, for the harmonious life, work and solidarity of groups, communities and nations.[28]

Other anarchists believed that by elaborating their ideal of anarchy they could usefully highlight the weaknesses of Marxist communism and, by warning the oppressed of its dangers, help secure genuine social revolution. Bakunin devoted considerable energy to teasing out the implications of Marx's communism, analysing his revolutionary programme in an effort to show that Marxist revolution would result in a reinforcement of state power, not its abolition.

These defences of utopianism reinforced the arguments of planners like Kropotkin and encouraged a broad range of anarchists to consider how they might develop their alternative. The organizational principle they developed is decentralized federation. This principle was first given shape by Proudhon. His view, as George Woodcock explains, was that

> the federal principle should operate from the simplest level of society. The organization of administration should begin locally and as near the direct control of the people as possible; individuals should start the process by federating into communes and association. Above that primary level the confederal organization would become less an organ of administration than of coordination between local units. Thus the nation would be replaced by a geographical confederation of regions, and Europe would become a confederation of confederations, in which the interest of the smallest province would have as much expression as that of the largest, and in which all affairs would be settled by mutual agreement, contract, and arbitration.[29]

Proudhon initially considered decentralized federation as a stepping-stone to anarchy rather than as an expression of anarchist organization. Yet taken up by other anarchists, it has come to be regarded as the framework for anarchist organization. Naturally, subsequent generations of anarchists have added their own glosses to Proudhon's ideas. One line of development was inspired by industrial development. In 1869 Jean-Louis Pindy proposed a system of dual federation, in which parallel communal and worker associations were integrated into one self-regulating system. James Guillaume elaborated a similar plan. Guillaume's version suggested a formal organizational framework in which the relationships between federal bodies, based on reciprocity and contract, were co-ordinated through banks of exchange. It also included a Communal Statistical Commission to 'gather and classify all statistical information pertaining to the commune' and perform other 'functions that are today exercised by the civil state' – including the registration of births and deaths (not marriage in a free society).[30] The central task of the agency was to ensure the uniform provision of goods and services across a region. Amongst other things, it could determine hours of work, exchange values and production targets for 'corporative' worker federations.

Anarcho-communist models of decentralized federation tended to be far more fluid than Guillaume's. For example, Reclus imagined that social relationships would be based on fraternity rather than contract, that groups would associate for particular purposes and that they would assume different forms. Reclus also imagined that these associations would emerge and disappear as their purposes arose and were met. Although his model did not preclude co-ordination, he believed that this would result from a sense of shared responsibility and that it would not require any formal decision-making structure. Modern international networks like People's Global Action (PGA) and the World Social Forum (WSF) follow similar principles, prioritizing co-ordination based on solidarity or affinity over contract and explicitly rejecting the notion of governmental, confessional or judicial function, providing instead a platform for plural, open discussion.

The two sketches of anarchy outlined below contrast an anarcho-syndicalist with an eco-anarchist view of anarchy. Neither, of course, is typical. The first is adapted from G.P. Maximoff's *Program of Anarcho-Syndicalism*, first published in 1927 to discuss the ways in which anarchists should address the problems of organization posed by the Bolshevik revolution. The second is taken from Graham Purchase's *My Journey With Aristotle to the Anarchist Utopia*. This literary utopia reworks the federalist idea to develop a communitarian and ecological, quasi-primitivist vision of anarchy.

anarcho-syndicalism: maximoff[31]

The leading idea of Maximoff's anarchy was the '*syndicalization* of production'. This process involved the transfer of the ownership of the industrial structure from employers to workers, organized in fully autonomous industrial unions, and the construction of producer-consumer communes. Like Guillaume, Maximoff argued for a large and permanent federal structure. Though he envisaged that unions would be organized on a local level and that they would be directly responsible for the management of production, he also believed that they would associate with other bodies in three further tiers of organization: production associations, unions of production associations (from different communes) and finally the General Congresses of Labour – or Council of Peoples' Economy and Culture. Each of these tiers of organization would be comprised of delegates from the body immediately below it.

Maximoff identified agriculture as the most important branch of industry and planned for the full socialization of production and cultivation of land. However, in the medium term he suggested that anarchists should be flexible and allow for agricultural production to be conducted on individual and co-operative, as well as communist, lines. Even in the long term, he argued that the Association of Peasant Communes – affiliated to the Confederation of Labour – would determine the precise utilization of land. Yet his hope was that agricultural workers could be encouraged to work collectively in groups.

With the socialization of land and labour, Maximoff imagined the integration of agriculture and industry in the creation of 'agro-industrial units'. The purpose of these units was to industrialize agriculture – to streamline food production – rather than to green industry. Although Maximoff was keen to avoid the development of vast agricultural units and recommended that the normal size would be 'an association of ten peasant farms', he was also keen to introduce more efficient, intensive methods of agricultural production. One area ripe for industrialization was cattle-rearing. Here, without wanting to force anyone to relinquish a treasured way of life, Maximoff observed that 'nomadic cattle raisers' would have to be brought up to live in a 'higher cultural environment' and at least 'to the level of present-day Russian peasants'.

One of the advantages of the agro-industrial units was that they provided workers with the opportunity to vary their labour. Maximoff admitted that some units would be comprised of workers who worked continuously in only one branch of the economy. Yet he believed that the principle of syndicalized production was 'freedom of labour, i.e. everybody's right to choose freely the type of activity most attractive to him, and the right to change freely from one type of work to another'. And for the most part Maximoff believed that the creation of these agro-industrial units would allow workers to move from agricultural labour to industry in accordance with seasonal changes and the needs of the economy.

All other branches of the economy – mines, heavy industry, public services – would also be syndicalized. The management of each area – communications, utilities, housing, transport and so on – would be transferred to the union of workers in that area and, through that transfer, each would be integrated into the communist economy. At the centre of the economy would be the Bank for Cash-and-Goods Credit. Like Guillaume, Maximoff believed that a Central Statistical Bureau would be necessary for the smooth running of the economy, but he charged the Bank with its operation. As well as monitoring information for distribution and exchange, the Bank would serve as the 'organic liaison' between the syndicates and the agricultural units and between the communist economy and the 'individualist world abroad'. The Bank would have considerable power and would be used in the immediately post-revolutionary period to encourage socialization in agriculture by means of credit and interest policy. The Bank would also have an accounting role in organizing distribution. However, everyday distribution would be handled by special agencies, organized in cities and villages by consumers' communes. Maximoff's idea was that free factories, workshops and agricultural units would deliver their products (only the surplus in the case of the agricultural units) to public warehouses and these in turn would pass on goods to the Bank. Until a system of needs could be established, Maximoff also envisaged that workers would receive tokens in return for their goods. But he gave some consideration to non-workers and insisted that communes make provision for 'the children, the nursing mothers, the old, the invalids and the sick'.

Maximoff recommended his plan of organization on the grounds that it offered a 'process of production on the basis of technical concentration and administrative decentralization'. When it came to administration, he argued that the economic organization of the syndicates would work alongside the organization of local communes and federations of communes. These units would protect individuals from tyranny and guard against the bureaucrat-ization of the economic system. In this hope, Maximoff argued:

> the communal confederation, constituted by thousands of freely acting labor organizations, removes all opportunities for the limita-tion of liberty and free activity. It definitely prevents the possibility

of dictatorship by any class, and, consequently, the possibility of
establishing a regime of terror. The basic character of the communal
confederation is such that it need have no fear of the widest freedom
of rights for all men, independent of their social origin, so long as
they work. As a result, true democracy, developed to its logical
extreme, can become a reality only under the conditions of a communal confederation. This democracy is Anarchy.[32]

Graham Purchase presents a very different vision.

eco-anarchy: Purchase[33]

Purchase outlines an imaginary society – a vision of a possible world
rather than a plan for organization. He outlines this vision in story
form about Tom, an Australian worker who, in the course of a
miners' strike is badly beaten up by police, and left for dead. Tom
regains consciousness in a third millennial eco-anarchist world,
brought into being by a second millennium Social-Ecological
Revolution. The state has been destroyed and the new world is
divided into ecological regions, distinguished from each other on
the basis of physiography, climate and culture. Tom's guide to the
world is Aristotle, an aged wise man (and friend of Plato). Aristotle
does not claim that the future is perfect. Indeed, he does not approve
of all the changes that have been made in the 1000 years between
Tom's beating and his reawakening. Moreover, he endorses Tom's
comment that 'nature and society are always evolving ... [t]here can
be no blue-print or unalterable plan of action ...'. Yet, like Old
Hammond in William Morris's utopian novel, *News From Nowhere*,
Aristotle serves as an intellectual conduit between the old and new
worlds and it is principally through him that Tom learns about and
reflects upon the future.

The society in which Tom finds himself is a half-way house
between social ecology and primitivism. The story is set in and
around Bear City. The city dominates the eco-region but from Tom's
original vantage point on a hillside it looks like a walled medieval
city and is small enough 'to be taken in in one single view'. Tom
learns that the walls serve only to protect the citizens from the local
wildlife and that they are not fortified to resist attack. The city was
established as part of a 'Bio-Regional Wilderness Reclamation
Project' and is set in forest and untamed wilderness. The citizens do
not try to seal themselves off from their environment. Indeed, they

have provided routes into the city – 'wild-life corridors' – that lead to a central park, passable by all but the largest and most dangerous creatures. They also allow bears to fish any one of the three rivers which run through the city, but they discourage these bears and the local lions from living in their midst. The city is fully self-sufficient and restricts the exploitation of the surrounding forest to the gathering of medicinal herbs, fishing and hunting trips, and the organization of camping holidays and wilderness camps for sick and handicapped children.

The dominant feature of Bear City is its ingenious application of sophisticated biotechnology. This technology enables the city to function self-sufficiently without damaging the eco-system. Aristotle tells Tom that Bear City has pioneered the 'science of edible chemurgy' and that everything in the city is edible. In the suburbs, for example, the citizens grow vegetables under cold frames made out of a 'membrane of clear plant extract' which dissolves into liquid plant food. And they live in remarkable energy efficient houses. From a distance, Bear City gleams as if constructed from glass and mirrors. When he enters the city Tom discovers that the house fronts are made from a reflective material that is used to maximize the amount of light that the solar energy panels, placed on the front of each house, can collect. This material is an important energy source in its own right. Each house has two sheets placed together like double-glazing but in a partially a sealed unit, which allows water to flow though, and energy-converting algae to live in the gap. Houses, bicycles and, as Tom discovers later on in his journey, clothes and underwear are fully edible. The only thing that prevents the city from being eaten by rats and mice is the foul tasting vegetable lacquer that the inhabitants use to coat fixtures and fittings.

The citizens of Bear City live in considerable comfort. Citizens make use of botanochemical computers, televisions and phones and social ecology gives them a number of sources of energy: wood, gas, wind-power and micro-hydroelectric power to run these devices. The city has a complex underground road system for the use of botanochemical bicycles. It has a light railway network, for heavy freight, and a monorail passenger transport system connecting the city to neighbouring areas. It has access to a helicopter 'in emergencies' and has even developed a 'space-craft constructed entirely out of plant extracts'. Aristotle's daughter, Mollie, tells Tom that the rocket is still experimental and that the botanochemicals of which it is made are not expected to withstand much more than the heat of lift-off. Nonetheless, Mollie is optimistic about the possibilities of replacing 'metal alloys and ceramics' in space. Tom embraces both the ease of life and the technology that supports it. Still, Alex, Mollie's companion, is keen to defend Bear City's reliance on 'use-tools':

> 'How can we escape technology? The boomerang, the bulldozer and the botanochemical are just different technologies for different times or places, all of which are equally sophisticated in their own way. The tool is a defining feature of our species and without it we would not be human. The two important things are not to become entrapped by a particular technology and to acknowledge that any tool which damages the environment can no longer be used as a use-tool. A tool is by definition something that is useful. I suppose that a tool may be harmful in one instance and a use-tool in another, but that is beside the point'. In any case it takes years to learn how to make a perfect arrow from a flint-stone ... To say that stone-age people did not have tools or technology is to insult them and to misrepresent the complexity and dexterity of their life and culture. Have you ever tried to make a boomerang come back?[34]

Not everyone Tom meets likes Bear City. Aristotle's friend Jack lives in the wilderness of Bear Forest and does not want to be part of a bio-organism, even though the wilderness is only an hour away from the city centre. Mollie and Alex are fed up with urban life and are considering retreating with their children to a less artificial environment but they can do this easily because Bear City is not typical. After the revolution, the inhabitants of each bio-region decided how to 're-integrate their life-styles, towns and cities with the regional ecology of their area'. Some areas opted for 'low-technology' solutions, relying on traditional 'rural land usages'. In contrast, Bear City's adjoining neighbourhoods, Cat Creek and the Bullawara Desert region, are both technology-averse. Aristotle tells Tom that the people of Cat Creek have an 'ideological commitment to the horse and cart'. When Tom visits the area at the end of his journey he finds himself 'confronted by ... romantic scenes from painters like ... Millet or Pissaro'. He is also reminded of William Morris but Aristotle tells him that the area has been modelled on ideas elaborated by the 'social-environmental geographer' Kropotkin: 'small scale simple technologies ... lighten the hard work associated with traditional peasant life'. The peoples of Bullawara are still further removed from technology and city-life. This area is settled by 'original native peoples' and 'non-native bio-regionalists' or 'neo-primitivists' who live side-by-side in a harmonious nomadic existence.

In its political and economic organization the new world has both communitarian and syndicalist features. Relations between Bear City and the other neighbourhoods in the bio-region are informal. Mollie explains that since the neighbouring areas 'share the same river systems' they organize 'regular inter-regional watershed councils as well as many other cultural, political, industrial and interest-related gatherings of one kind or another'. Tom does not stay long enough in the future to witness any disputes between these areas, but is told by Jack that from time to time violence and fighting occur. When this happens, mediators like Aristotle facilitate the resolution of disputes by bringing the parties together so that they can find consensual solutions to their problems.

There is no property in 'public or civic goods'. For example, bicycles line the road tunnels, freely available for common use. Bear City is run on a system of simple exchange. There is no money in the economy and no attempt is made to assess the value of work. Mollie's friend Peter calls the system 'social anarchism'. Some regions have more formal voucher arrangements, much as Guillaume and Maximoff envisaged, but in Bear City people give and take according to need. Goods are brought to and taken from warehouses. A simple computerized database keeps a check on supply and demand. Whilst this local database ensures that overproduction and scarcity are a thing of the past a more sophisticated database, called Reclus, provides information – available in schools – about the regional management of eco-systems. Life is lived communally. Whilst all houses have their own kitchens, most people prefer to use the more efficient communal facilities. Work is organized on a voluntary basis. There is still a division between domestic and non-domestic labour, but the performance of work is not gendered (Tom is told that 'old people who can't get around too much' look after kitchens and gardens). Domestic chores are reduced to a minimum since composting has replaced the need for most washing and washing up. Non-domestic workers organize themselves in syndicates. These syndicates represent all the most important services and industries and operate on a worldwide basis. Aristotle tells Tom that Bear City is the world centre for Cycology – the Bike syndicate. But Tom also learns of a variety of others: the Teacher's Syndicate, the Builder's Syndicate, Mechanical Engineer's Syndicate, the Astronautical and Satellite Maintenance

Syndicate (of which Mollie is a part) and less conventionally, the Toy and Treats Syndicate and the Sexual Auxiliaries Syndicate, dedicated to the production of condoms made from 'an unbelievably thin material'. All these syndicates have branch organizations in the different regions, but workers in all syndicates consider themselves to be part of 'one big union'.

Like Morris's *News From Nowhere*, Purchase's anarchy is populated with beautiful, intelligent and happy characters. But his descriptions of social life in Bear City suggest that the inspiration for his utopia comes from the 1960s as much as from Morris's classic. On his first night in Bear City, Tom drifts off to sleep in a drug-induced haze, having smoked copious amounts of 'good' marijuana with his hosts. Similarly, Tom is delighted to find that heterosexuality is the convention of Bear City and that its women are reluctant to wear too much of the thin, edible clothing available to them. He's equally pleased to discover that the first woman he propositions is only too happy to grapple with his heavy denims and share her product-awareness of the Sexual Auxiliaries Syndicate. Mollie refers to nine-teenth-century anarchism as 'austere'. Yet for all its hippy overtones and primitivist leanings, Purchase's social ecology retains some of the character of this earlier work. The citizens of Bear City can only choose to spend their time 'making love in the forest or ... dedicating [their] lives to a space program' because life is governed by the 'rational organization of things' – a very nineteenth-century concept. In a final echo of early anarchist thought, Purchase pins the success of social anarchism on the operation of a (neutral and non-oppressive) statistical agency. Though this is computerized, it appears, neverthe-less, to pose the same problems as Maximoff's Central Bureau.

Like Maximoff's anarcho-syndicalist model, Purchase's utopia emerges from a specific set of debates and it engages with them in order to show how anarchist theory might be translated into prac-tice. An alternative way of illustrating the potential for anarchy is to design forms of action that embrace anarchist principles. This third approach is discussed in the next section.

experiments in anarchy

Anarchists have attempted to apply their principles of organization in a number of fields. This section considers two areas of activity: anarcho-syndicalism and anarchist communitarianism. These two well-tested fields of action raise important questions about scope of anarchy, democratic decision-making and, picking up the point from the previous chapter, the potential to realize liberty in community.

anarcho-syndicalism

Anarcho-syndicalists argue that there is direct and intimate relationship between the struggle against capitalism and the organization of anarchy. For Ferdinand Pelloutier, the founder of the school, syndicalism was a vehicle for anarchy. Anarchists, he argued, should not wait for a revolutionary situation before developing alternative economic systems. To the contrary, if they were to succeed in organizing production and distribution, workers should develop these systems in the body of capitalism. The commitment to build an anarchist alternative to capitalism through syndicalist organization remains the central tenet of the modern anarcho-syndicalist movement. The British Section of the International Workers Association, the Solidarity Federation (SolFed), encourages association in 'locals'. Locals provide a platform for anti-racist, anti-sexist and environmental campaigns in both community and workplace. They spread information in meetings, through bulletins, leaflets and the web, thus encouraging the development of more locals. In the workplace, members of locals working in the same sector form 'networks' to promote worker solidarity and improve working conditions. And the aim of this activity is to build the framework for anarchy:

> As Locals and Networks grow, they practise community and workers' self-management. Eventually, industries will be run by producers and consumers. In other words, by workers (in Networks) and people in the wider community (Locals) who want the goods and services they provide. And this is not flight of fancy or text-book dream. As the solidarity movement grows in members and influence, so does the scope for action.[35]

Assessments of anarcho-syndicalism have often revolved around the experience of the Spanish Confederación Nacional del Trabajo (CNT), especially in the period leading up to and including the Civil War (1936–39). There are several reasons for this. First, the CNT is one of only a few revolutionary syndicalist organizations to identify with anarchism. In the late nineteenth and early twentieth centuries enthusiasm for syndicalism swept through Europe, Scandinavia, Canada and across the Americas. Yet most of the resulting organizations prioritized working-class unity over ideological commitment. Indeed, the member's pocket book for the US International Workers of the World (IWW or Wobblies) includes the following resolution:

> That to the end of promoting industrial unity and of securing necessary discipline within the organization, the IWW refuses all alliances, direct and indirect, with existing political parties or anti-political sects, and disclaims responsibility for any individual opinion or act which may be at variance with the purposes herein expressed.[36]

The founding congress of Belles Artes in 1910 defined the CNT in similarly neutral terms. The CNT was designed to help the working class 'gain its complete freedom, by means of the revolutionary expropriation of the bourgeoisie'.[37] Yet a significant number of militants within the CNT understood that revolutionary action implied a commitment to anarchy and the milieu within which the CNT operated was shaped by anarchist ideas. At the 1936 Zaragoza conference the CNT accepted a detailed plan for anarcho-communist organization as the basis for revolutionary action.

The CNT was also a powerful organization. At its peak, it had an estimated 800,000 members. Moreover, it had a well-developed federal structure, and although there were arguments within the CNT about the priority attached to industrial federation or local autonomy, it remained an effective focus for revolutionary action. Above all, in the revolution prompted by the outbreak of the Spanish Civil War, the CNT got the opportunity to test the practicality of anarchist principles of organization.

Anarchists evaluating the CNT's civil war experience fall into one or two strongly contrasting camps. Its staunchest defenders acknowledge weaknesses in the CNT's programmes of land collectivization and worker self-management, admit that some sectors of the economy worked better than others and that the co-ordination of economic activity was dogged by serious problems. But in Catalonia – and Barcelona in particular, where the CNT predominated – they also argue that the workers proved themselves more than capable of taking control of the economic apparatus. In the first days of the civil war, workers provided arms and ammunitions for militias, as well as milk and bread for citizens. As the revolution grew, transport and health services, food and textile industries were all managed efficiently. In some areas of the economy – Peirats highlights baking – CNT members managed to improve on pre-revolutionary standards of production. As importantly, the workers accomplished their ends democratically, through self-management. Kevin Doyle of the Workers' Solidarity Movement believes that anti-globalizers can learn a lot from their example. The Spanish workers, he argues, provided 'one of the best examples of how alternatives to capitalism can actually function and thrive'.[38] How can their success be explained? Mintz is unequivocal:

> For us it is unquestionably the structure of the CNT and the inter-
> nationalist outlook it imbued in its militants which explains this speed
> of organisation. Even if the lectures, pamphlets and books explaining
> the ideas of libertarian communism were simplistic they were
> adequate and, without pretending to offer easy solutions for every-
> thing, they convinced the militants of the need to respond quickly to
> the possibilities of the situation with initiative and creativity.[39]

In the second group, critics acknowledge the revolutionary achievements of CNT in Barcelona and elsewhere, but question the extent to which syndicalism can be credited with the revolution's achievements. Bookchin suggests that the limited success of the wartime experiment was the result of independent initiatives taken by workers, outside the organizational framework of the CNT, and not as a consequence of syndicalism. Moreover, whilst he argues that the CNT leadership included many moderates keen to keep the revolution in check, he locates the weaknesses of the CNT in its 'economistic' outlook, not the political foibles of these personalities. In 1907, in famous debate with Pierre Monatte, Malatesta described the relation-ship between anarchism and syndicalism in the form of the equation: anarchism > syndicalism.[40] Bookchin adopts a similar view. Like all syndicalist movements, the CNT wrongly prioritized the struggle of the industrial workers and confused the ability to control production with the construction of anarchy. The 'high regard that the factory system imposes on the workers, proved fatal'. He continues:

> In areas influenced by the CNT, the workers did indeed, 'expropriate'
> the economy ... But 'workers' control' ... did not produce a 'new
> society'. The underlying idea that by controlling much of the
> economy the anarcho-syndicalist movement would essentially
> control the society ... proved a myth'.[41]

The history of the Spanish Civil War and the tragedy of the revolution's defeat make these discussions of the CNT highly emotive. Yet it's important to remember that the point at issue here is not the heroism or courage of Spanish workers in the face of fascist onslaught, but the breadth of the anarchist vision. The historical argument leaves little room for compromise: anarchy is either about finding ways to secure the workers' direct control of production and distribution or it's about something else. The anarcho-syndicalist position is very clear. Modern alternatives suggest greater ambition, but appear more diffuse.

anarchist communitarianism

Anarchist communitarianism operates in two spheres: intentional community and community networking. Intentional community describes an experiment in anarchist community-living and like much else in anarchism it dates back to the nineteenth century. Community networking is a more recent phenomenon, blossoming in the 1960s. Networkers often argue that anarchy should not be regarded as a pristine model or mere counterpoint to the state, and that it should be seen instead as a constantly evolving movement, embracing an attitude to social life realized through the adoption of certain principles of organization and 'permanent opposition'. Communitarians in this second group live in mainstream society but work in local organizations to advance an anarchist vision. Community networking thus offers an alternative to anarcho-syndicalism whilst working on the same principles: it is designed to encourage the creation of new, decentralized institutions in the body of capitalism, by focusing on neighbourhoods and localities rather than the workplace.

Yet anarchist communitarians share a commitment to an ideal of the good life defined by mutual support and reciprocity. Their ideal holds little appeal for right-libertarians who tend to identify the good life with independence, self-help and charity rather than interdependence, mutual aid and care and are prone to equate 'community' with 'local repression and narrow-minded intolerance'.[42] Of course, libertarians also imagine that anarchy is about social interaction, but their models of relationships are thin – 'modular' rather than organic – and tend to be posited on a primary defensive need to secure private property against potential transgression. Rothbard's basic unit of organization is the homestead: even the family appears too 'thick' an organization for the libertarian society. Indeed, there is no assumption of natural affection in this world: owners respond to their offspring rationally and where affection fails, sell them to those who really want them on the free market.

The first form of communitarianism, intentional community, has been a constant feature of anarchist activity since the 1890s, if not before. The first wave of anarchist community building is associated with the 'milieux libres' in France and campaigns like the 'New Australia Movement' – an organization created to settle 'healthy and intelligent men and women' disgruntled with life in the 'working man's Paradise' in co-operative communities in South America.[43] These experiments were often short lived, but subsequent generations of anarchists have continued the tradition. Franco's victory in the Civil War encouraged groups of Spanish anarchists in exile to set up communities in France. And a general dissatisfaction with materialism acted as a catalyst for a wave of American experiments the following decade.

Intentional community is often associated with a desire for rural living. As Lerner argues, the post-war American movement reflected 'a response to dissatisfaction with the cities'.[44] Yet anarchist communities have been set up in urban as well as rural areas. Indeed, although it is usually regarded as anarchistic rather than anarchist, one of the best known experiments in intentional community – Christiania or 'Freetown' – is based in Copenhagen. Often, too, community is linked to Christian or ethical anarchism – Tolstoyans and other Christian anarchists played a leading part in both British and Dutch movements. However, communitarianism has engaged a wide spectrum of anarchists: from individualists to communists and from those seeking space to prepare for guerrilla warfare to those looking for an opportunity to create new ways of living.

One of the chief concerns of anarchists involved in intentional community is to show that individuals and groups can improve the quality of their social relations by removing themselves from the influence of mainstream culture. This concern is made explicit in the mission statement of the Anarchist Communitarian Network (ACN), an association set up to provide help and support to anarchist communitarians in America. The ACN describes intentional community as a movement 'discontent with the dominant norms of alienation, competition, and antagonism'. By encouraging anarchist experiments in community it hopes to foster 'a qualitative change of social relationships and institutions', making them 'non-hierarchical, democratic … intimate, and authentic'.

Anarchist observers of community have often testified to the success with which communitarians have realized this general goal. For example, when Augustin Souchy paid Spanish comrades a visit, he recorded the extraordinary conviviality of the group. Their settlement 'was an economic and cultural commune based on voluntarism after the pattern of the Spanish collectividades':

> Meals were served in a special communal dining room, laundry and clothing were allotted according to need and vacation money was disbursed from a common treasury just like in a happy family. Vacationers from outside gladly and voluntarily lent a helping hand in agricultural work. No written by-laws were needed. Every six months a chairman, treasurer and secretary were elected
>
> ... The French peasants in the neighborhood at first regarded the foreign colonists with suspicion but soon changed their attitude ... after a short time friendly and neighbourly relations were established. I could close the notes in my diary with the blunt sentence: 'Overall impression of the free collective of d'Aymare: positive'.[45]

Yet on two particular issues – democratic decision-making and individual liberty – for which intentional communities have provided a platform for analysis, the record of anarchist community appears less certain.

Discussions of democracy have tended to focus on the possibilities of consensus decision-making. The principle of consensus decision-making is straightforward: individuals come together, respecting each other as equal voices, to determine preferred courses of action by common agreement. The attraction of consensus decision-making is that it avoids the need for voting and seems, therefore, to offer a solution to the problem of majoritarianism. Specifically, in contrast to other systems of democracy (including the non-hierarchical, participatory, municipalist model developed by Bookchin), consensus decision-making does not allow minorities to be outvoted (coerced) by majorities. Yet as an alternative method of organizing anarchy, consensus decision-making is also problematic. Jo Freeman's critique of anarcha-feminism, the *Tyranny of Structurelessness*, points to the root of the difficultly:

> Any group of people of whatever nature coming together for any length of time for any purpose, will inevitably structure itself in some fashion. The structure may be flexible, it may vary over time, it may evenly or unevenly distribute tasks, power and resources over

the members of the group. But it will be formed regardless of the
abilities, personalities and intentions of the people involved. The
very fact that we are individuals with different talents, predispos-
itions and backgrounds makes this inevitable.[46]

Even in most convivial communities, individuals will organize
themselves in ways that advantage some members over others.
When it comes to decision-making, the more articulate, charismatic
or knowledgeable are likely to dominate. Moreover, where communities formally recognize the equality of members, the less able or
confident are open to the coercion of those who dominate. In
Freeman's terms: ' "structurelessness" becomes a way of masking
power'.

Libertarians like Rand have long attacked the idea of consensus
decision making, dubbing it as 'new fascism'. Others more
sympathetic to the principle have responded positively to critiques
like Freeman's. For example, the primary work of the New York
based Common Wheel Collective is to build up a picture of decision
making in community and show how its problems might be
addressed and corrected through practice. Their guide, the *Collective
Book on Collective Process*, explores in some detail 'democratic
process within collectives, focusing on the problems that develop
and possible approaches toward fixing those problems'.[47] Yet whilst
the Collective are upbeat about the possibility of finding anarchist
solutions to these problems, their work testifies to a widespread
experience of manipulation, obstruction and non-cooperation in
community.

These gloomy findings have been reinforced by Michael Taylor's
work. In *Community, Anarchy and Liberty* Taylor argues that anarchy
is possible only where relations between people are based on community. He defines community by three criteria: individuals must
share values and beliefs in common, their relationships must be
direct and complex and their social arrangements must be based on
reciprocity. Contrary to Bookchin and other anarchists, he argues
that it is possible to achieve liberty outside of community. However,
disentangling negative freedom (the idea of being prevented from
doing something) from autonomy (the idea of subjecting norms
and actions to review and rational deliberation) he argues that
community is compatible with liberty.

Taylor believes that one of the difficulties confronting anarchists
is to find a way of constructing communities that are not illiberal.

The achievement of his aim, whilst possible, is extremely difficult. The one context in which anarchy, liberty and community can co-exist is the 'secular family commune' – where groups attempt to institutionalize friendship in a domestic environment. Yet friendship is precarious as a basis for community and the aims of the secular family commune can be compromised if members of the community mistakenly treat the maintenance of the domestic environment as a measure of friendship, thus prioritizing the need to fulfil social duties over the more difficult task of building human relationships. Moreover, even where secular families succeed, Taylor argues that the prospect for anarchy is undermined by the difficulty of maintaining inter-community relations. Taylor does not believe that his inability to find a solution to this problem suggests that 'the goal of a radically decentralised world of small communities' is unattractive. Nevertheless, he concludes:

> We have no grounds for believing that growing up and living in community necessarily engenders a tolerant, pacific and cooperative disposition towards outsiders. It is true that many primitive anarchic communities lived at peace with their neighbours (though having little contact with them and invariably taking a dim view of them); but many did not, and the world is a great deal more crowded now.[48]

Experiments in anarchist communitarianism have not provided a robust answer to this objection. However, proponents of the second form of anarchist communitarianism – community networking – suggest that the objection can be met.

As Howard Ehrlich explains, the purpose of networking is to build 'a "transfer culture"', to extend anarchist ideas by constructing sites for anarchy in mainstream society.[49] Unlike members of intentional communities, networkers are not separated from other members of the community: they work with them in order to rebuild social relationships on the basis of trust and support. Tom Knoche defines the project as:

> ... changing what we can do today and undoing the socialization process that has depoliticized so many of us. We can use it to build the infrastructure that can respond and make greater advances when our political and economic systems are in crisis and vulnerable to change.[50]

Networking embraces a wide range of activities – cultural, political and economic. In 1969, Kingsley Widmer identified networking with the furtherance of rebellious life-styles, institutional subversion and 'refusing': challenging the institutional order through radical criticism, 'the dissident way, the comic resistance, the emphatic difference, the intransigent act'.[51] As John Clark argues, networking has a '*psychosocial*' dimension. The purpose of waging this kind of struggle is to 'combat domination' and 'self-consciously seek to maintain ... personalistic human relationships'.[52]

In the 1970s, Giovanni Baldelli described the process of community networking as the mobilization of ethical capital. Today, many new anarchists draw on the image of the rhizome to capture a similar idea. Some anarchists like this idea because it emphasizes the ecological thrust of their experiments. Thus, the Rhizome collective in Texas is about bicycles, herbalism, edible landscaping, rain catching and 'sustainability community organizing'. For others, the rhizome is a metaphor for the plurality of the networking process. A debate in New Zealand about the renaming of an anarchist magazine includes an exchange between an activist preferring the title 'mycorhiza' (inspired by the 'symbiotic association of the mycelium of a fungus with the roots of certain plants') and another who suggests rhizome. The clinching argument is that rhizome is 'a very good analogy for anarchism' because 'it is a non-hierarchical roots system (i.e. anarchist grass roots ...) ... not just a term for something "ecological"'.[53]

Networks can be local, regional and even international. The Anarchist Black Cross, set up to help victims of Franco's oppression, is a network of support groups which assists prisoners all over the world to obtain basic human rights and fight against 'prisons and the poverty, racism and genocide that accompanies them'. Other tangible examples of networking include the establishment of housing and worker co-operatives, autonomous meeting centres – the Reithalle in Bern is one example – and participation in LET systems (local exchange currency systems). As Carol Ehrlich notes, networking has limitless possibilities:

> Developing alternative forms of organization means building self-help clinics, instead of fights to get one radical on a hospital's board of directors; it means women's video groups and newspapers, instead of commercial television and newspapers; living collectives, instead of isolated nuclear families; rape crisis centres; food co-ops;

parent-controlled day-care centres; free schools, printing co-ops; alternative radio groups, and so on.[54]

Recently anarchist anti-globalizers have associated community networking with the emergence of alternative economies. They point to the emergence of gift economies, living economies and local currency systems, to land reclamation projects undertaken by groups like Brazil's Landless Workers' Movement and programmes for sustainable and bio-diverse agriculture – for example, EcoVilla in Ecuador, to show how local experiments can provide a real alternative to corporate capitalism.[55] The enthusiasm with which European anarchists have greeted these experiments is often informed by an appreciation of their diversity and by a willingness to avoid automatically slotting them into frameworks of anarchist politics. In other cases, however, anarchists draw back to the anthropological arguments advanced by anarchists like Kropotkin and through the medium of 'natural anarchy' treat these experiments as examples of anarchy in action. The disagreement parallels the difference between those who understand the rhizome to describe a principle of organization and those who see it as a particular kind of eco-activity. Either way, there is a tendency within both positions to read anarchy into any network – to prioritize the movement over the goal.

Whereas intentional communities seek to develop anarchy in isolation from wider society, networks aim to extend anarchist practices in all areas of social life – in rural and urban, industrial environments. The problem posed by networking is not, as Taylor suggests, how to develop inter-communal relations, but to show that the networks themselves are anarchist in any significant sense. Some anarchists have detected a potential fuzziness in networking theory. Only a year after embracing 'refusal' as a form of anarchist protest, Kingsley Widmer wrote in *Anarchy*:

> Our sympathy for countering culture should remain this side of the populist murkiness of the protesting young and its unpromising wooziness and passivity. Any critical effort suggests that we won't get a 'political end' without some sort of 'political means'. Certainly we need a radical change in sensibility, but if it does not include social and political effectiveness it will not end as a change at all.[56]

The difficulty to which Widmer points, has manifested itself in political as well as cultural spheres of action. In particular, debates between anarcha-feminists suggest that networking can blunt anarchist ideas rather than extend them. In the late 1960s and '70s anarcha-feminists often made common cause with radical feminists who, like them, eschewed campaigns for equal rights in the belief that the causes of oppression could only be overcome by the transformation of social relations in the domestic as well as the public sphere. The arguments resonated across a wide spectrum of local women's groups. As Peggy Kornegger argues, women's groups 'frequently reflected an unspoken libertarian consciousness'. The rebellion was 'against the competitive power games, impersonal hierarchy, and mass organization tactics of male politics'. Women organized themselves 'into small, leaderless, consciousness-raising (C-R) groups, which dealt with personal issues in our daily lives'.[57]

Such was the coincidence of anarchist views and feminist practice that anarcha-feminists were encouraged to believe that the decentralized structure of the women's movement was a sign of its inherent anarchism. In 1974, Lynne Farrow boldly asserted that '[f]eminism practises what Anarchism preaches. One might go as far as to claim feminists are the only existing protest groups that can honestly be called practising Anarchists'.[58] Writing the following year, Peggy Kornegger declared with equal confidence: 'feminists have been unconscious anarchists in both theory and practice for years'.

L. Susan Brown has recently questioned this view and argued that the relationship between anarchism and feminism has been overstated. Just as Malatesta described anarchism to be greater than syndicalism, Brown objects that whilst '[a]narchism must be feminist if it is to remain self-consistent', not all feminists are anarchists.[59] In their defence, neither Farrow nor Kornegger argued that all feminists were anarchists. Rather, they insisted that the feminist movement had demonstrated a potential for anarchy that anarcha-feminists could harness. From their perspective, anarcha-feminists did not need to know that the women involved in their networks were committed to realizing anarchy. The point was to engage in activity that was consistent with this goal.

Yet it's not clear from this position whether networking requires any specifically anarchist input and, if so, what that might be. Ehrlich's view is that anarchists must be satisfied that there is a purpose to their action and that they should test proposals against five conditions. Each activity must:

1. offer 'a genuine service ... in an openly politicized context'. In particular, networking must be based on decentralized control and worker self-management;

2. operate on collective principles;
3. introduce means of self-assessment and criticism;
4. mount educational programmes – particularly in 'issues of political struggle';
5. directly challenge and assault the equivalent state structures that the alternative seeks to replace or make redundant.[60]

Provided the action meets these conditions, then any kind of alternative institution – be it a co-operative venture or a worker-managed business – can be used as a platform for anarchist communitarianism. Other communitarians go further to suggest that the subject and success of community actions are less important than the process of engagement. For example, John Schumacher argues 'the making is never over – the making *is* community'. He quotes David Wieck: 'nothing secures anarchist society, whether of large extent or of commune-size or consisting of two persons, except *continuous realization* of the human potential for free engagement and disagreement'.[61] It's difficult to see how this approach usefully addresses existing asymmetries of power.

summary

This chapter has examined three ways in which anarchists have attempted to outline their visions of anarchy. It looked first at arguments about 'primitive' or preliterate ways of life and examined the ways in which anarchists have evaluated traditional societies as models for anarchy. The second section discussed a variety of anarchist responses to utopianism and outlined two utopias: Maximoff's anarcho-syndicalist model and Graham Purchase's eco-anarchy. Finally, the chapter reviewed examples of practical anarchy – anarcho-syndicalism and community. In the post-war period, communitarians have consciously developed their models of anarchy as alternatives to anarcho-syndicalism. Yet Souchy's observations of the conviviality of Spanish anarcho-syndicalists, on the one hand, and the willingness of anti-globalizers to reflect on the organizational potential of local networking initiatives, on the other, suggests that there might be relationship between the two. If they are treated as alternative choices, there is a danger that the intuitive appeal of anarchy will exist in an inverse relation to the clarity of its objectives.

further reading

Giovanni Baldelli, *Social Anarchism* (Chicago, New York: Aldine Atherton, 1971)

Mark Bevir, 'The Rise of Ethical Anarchism in Britain, 1885–1900', *Historical Research: Bulletin of the Institute of Historical Research*, 69 (169): 143–63

Burnett Bolloten, *The Spanish Revolution* (Chapel Hill: University of North Carolina Press, 1979)

Alfredo Bonanno, *Critique of Syndicalist Methods* (London: Bratach Dubn, n.d.), also at http://www.geocities.com

Sharif Gemie, 'Counter-Community: An Aspect of Anarchist Political Culture', *Journal of Contemporary History*, 29: 349–67

Robert Graham, 'Reinventing Hierarchy: The Political Theory of Social Ecology', *Anarchist Studies*, 12 (1), 2004: 16–35

Gaston Leval, *Collectives in the Spanish Revolution*, http://dwardmac. pitzer.edu/anarchist_archives

Peter Kropotkin, *Fields, Factories and Workshops*, http://dwardmac. pitzer.edu/anarchist_archives

Peter Kropotkin, *Mutual Aid: A Factor of Evolution*, http://dwardmac. pitzer.edu/anarchist_archives

Marcel van der Linden and Wayne Thorpe (eds), *Revolutionary Syndicalism* (Hants., England: Scolar Press, 1990)

Stephen Marshall, 'Christiania', The Planning Factory, 10, http://www.bartlett.ucl.ac.uk/planning.information/PF/ PFIO.html#Christiania

George Molnar, 'Conflicting Strains in Anarchist Thought', in C. Ward (ed.) *A Decade of Anarchy* (London: Freedom Press, 1987), 24–36

William Morris, *News From Nowhere*, ed. D. Leopold (Oxford: Oxford University Press, 2003)

Tadzio Mueller, 'Empowering Anarchy: Power, Hegemony and Anarchist Strategy', *Anarchist Studies*, 11 (2): 122–49

José Peirats, *The CNT In The Spanish Revolution*, vol. 1 (Hastings, East Sussex: Meltzer Press, 2001)

Jeff Stein, 'Some Thoughts on Building An Anarchist Movement', *Social Anarchism*, 26, 1998, http://library.nothingness.org/ articles/SA/en/display/250

Vernon Richards, *Lessons of the Spanish Revolution* (London: Freedom Press, 1983)

links

Anarchist Black Cross: www.anarchistblackcross.org.
Anarchist Communitarian Network: http://anarchistcommunitarian.
    net/missionstatement.shtml
Christiania, Copenhagen: www.Christiania.org
Peoples' Global Action: http://www.nadir.org/initiative/agp.cocha/
    principles.htm
Practical Anarchy: http://www.practicalanarchy.org
Reithalle, Bern: http://www.reitschule.ch/reitschule
Thrall (non-sectarian collective – magazine for Aotearoa/New Zea-
    land): http://www.thrall.orcon.net.nz/
World Social Forum: www.wsfindia.org/charter/php

notes

1. K. Maddock, 'Primitive Societies and Social Myths' in C. Ward, *A Decade of Anarchy* (London: Freedom Press, 1987), 70.
2. P. Kropotkin, *Mutual Aid: A Factor of Evolution* (Boston, Mass: Extending Horizons Books, 1902).
3. P. Kropotkin, *Revolutionary Pamphlets*, R. Balwin (ed.), (New York: Dover, 1970), 92.
4. H. Barclay, *The State* (London: Freedom Press, 2003), 92.
5. M. Bookchin, *The Modern Crisis* (Philadelphia: New Society Publishers, 1986), 26.
6. M. Bookchin, *The Ecology of Freedom* (Palo Alto, California: Cheshire Books, 1982), 279.
7. J. Zerzan, *Running on Emptiness* (Los Angeles: Feral House, 2002), 71; 152.
8. Zerzan, *Running on Emptiness*, 5.
9. Zerzan, *Running on Emptiness*, 49.
10. F. Perlman, *Against His-tory, Against Leviathan!* (Detroit: Black & Red, 1983), 9–10.
11. H. Barclay, *People Without Government* (London: Kahn & Averill/Cienfuegos, 1982), 12.
12. Barclay, *The State*, 100.
13. T. Tuiono, 'Tino Rangatiratanga and Capitalism', *Thrall*, 24: 6–7, http://www.illegalvoices.org/apoc.knowledge.articles.ideas.teanu.htm
14. M. Bakunin, *On Anarchism*, S. Dolgoff (ed.) (Montreal: Black Rose, 1980), 193; 207; 395.
15. J. Pilgrim, 'Anarchism and Stateless Societies', *Anarchy* 58, 5 (2): 367.

16. G. Woodcock, *Anarchism and Anarchists* (Kingston, Ontario: Quarry Press, 1982), 258–9.
17. P. Kropotkin, *Fields, Factories and Workshops* (London: Thomas Nelson & Sons, 1898).
18. J. Fliss, 'What is Primitivism?' http://primitivism.com/what-is-primitivism.htm
19. L. Tolstoy, *Government is Violence*, D. Stephens (ed.) (London: Phoenix Press, 1990), 128.
20. *Black Flag*, 'Technology, Capitalism and Anarchism', http://flag.blackened.net/blackflag/219/219techn.htm
21. N. Rosenblum, introduction to *Thoreau: Political Writings* (Cambridge: Cambridge University Press, 1996), x.
22. M.L. Berneri, *Journey Through Utopia* (London: Freedom Press, 1982), 3.
23. R. Rocker, *Anarcho-Syndicalism* (London: Phoenix Press, n.d.), 20.
24. J. McQuinn, *What is Ideology?*, http://primitivism.com/ideology/htm
25. Bookchin, *The Modern Crisis*, 7.
26. N. Bukharin, 'Anarchy and Scientific Communism', in the *Poverty of Statism* (Orkney: Cienfuegos Press, 1981), 3.
27. G. Pleckhanov, *Anarchism and Socialism* (Chicago: Charles H. Kerr, n.d.), 127.
28. G. Landauer, *For Socialism* (St Louis, Missouri: Telos Press, 1978), 54.
29. G. Woodcock, *Anarchism* (Harmondsworth: Penguin, 1979), 130.
30. J. Guillaume, in D. Guérin (ed.), *No Gods, No Masters*, vol. 1 (Edinburgh: AK Press, 1998), 219.
31. G.P. Maximoff, *Program of Anarcho-Syndicalism* (Sydney: Monty Miller Press, 1985).
32. Maximoff, *Program of Anarcho-Syndicalism*, 43.
33. G. Purchase, *My Journey With Aristotle to the Anarchist Utopia* (Gualala, California: III Publishing, 1994).
34. Purchase, *My Journey*, 73–4.
35. SolFed, *Who Is Solidarity Federation?* http://www.solfed.force9.co.uk/sf.htm
36. IWW *Preamble and Constitution* (Chicago: IWW, 1972), 45.
37. J. Peirats, *Anarchists in the Spanish Revolution* (Detroit: Black & Red, 1977), 28.
38. K. Doyle, *The Anarchist Economic Alternative to Globalisation*, http://flag.blackened.net.revolt.talks.global100html
39. F. Mintz, 'The Spanish Labour Movement' in A. Meltzer (ed.), *A New World in Our Hearts* (Orkney: Cienfuegos Press, 1978).
40. J. Maitron, *Le Mouvement Anarchiste En France*, vol. 1 (Paris: François Maspero, 1975), 327.
41. M. Bookchin, 'The Ghost of Anarcho-Syndicalism', *Anarchist Studies*, 1 (1): 18.

42.　J. Baker, 'Question Regulation!' in J. Baker and J. Peacott, *Regulated to Death: Anarchist Arguments Against Government Regulation in Our Lives* (Boston: BAD Press, 1992), 8.

43.　New Australia Movement, Letter to *Freedom*, http://anarchistcommunitarian. net/articles/refoncom.kroadv.shtml

44.　M. Lerner, 'Anarchism and the American Counter-Culture' in J. Joll and D. Apter (eds), *Anarchism Today* (London & Basingstoke: Macmillan Press, 1971), 40.

45.　A. Souchy, *Beware Anarchist!* (Chicago: Charles H. Kerr, 1992), 157.

46.　J. Freeman, *The Tyranny of Structurelessness*, http://www.illegalvoices.org/ apoc/heat/tools/freeman.html

47.　Common Wheel Collective, *Collective Book on Collective Process*, http://www.geocities.com/collectivebook

48.　M. Taylor, *Community, Anarchy and Liberty* (Cambridge: Cambridge University Press, 1982), 167.

49.　H. Ehrlich, 'How to Get From Here to There: Building Revolutionary Transfer Culture', in Ehrlich (ed.), *Reinventing Anarchy Again* (Edinburgh: AK Press, 1996), 331.

50.　T. Knoche, 'Organizing Communities' in H. Ehrlich (ed.), *Reinventing Anarchy Again*, 352.

51.　K. Widmer, 'On Refusing' in C. Ward (ed.), *A Decade of Anarchy* (London: Freedom Press, 1978), 96.

52.　J. Clark, *The Anarchist Moment* (Montreal: Black Rose, 1983), 31–2.

53.　bobo, 'the point', http://www.anarchism.org.nz.node/view/985

54.　C. Ehrlich 'Socialism, Anarchism and Feminism' in H. Ehrlich (ed.), *Reinventing Anarchy Again*, 175.

55.　http://docs.indymedia.org/view/Global/AlternativesFeature

56.　K. Widmer, 'Counter-Culture', *Anarchy*, 109, 10 (3): 82.

57.　P. Kornegger, 'Anarchism: the feminist connection', in H. Ehrlich (ed.), *Reinventing Anarchy Again*, 159.

58.　L. Farrow, 'Feminism as Anarchism', *Quiet Rumours* (London: Dark Star, n.d.), 11.

59.　L.S. Brown, 'Beyond Feminism: Anarchism and Human Freedom', in H. Ehrlich (ed.), *Reinventing Anarchy Again*, 153.

60.　H. Ehrlich, 'The Logic of Alternative Institutions', in H. Ehrlich, C. Ehrlich, D. de Leon and G. Morris (eds) *Reinventing Anarchy* (London: Routledge & Kegan Paul, 1979), 346.

61.　J. Schulmacher, 'Communal Living: Making Community', *Social Anarchism*, 25, 1998, http://library.nothingness.org/articles.SA. en.display.135.

strategies for change

It is up to each committed person to take responsibility for stopping the exploitation of the natural world ... If not you who, if not now when?
(Earth Liberation Front,
http://earthliberation front.com/about)

Do not let anyone tell you that we are only a tiny handful, too weak ever to attain the grand objective at which we aim ... All we who suffer and who are outraged, we are an immense crowd; we are an ocean in which all could be submerged. As soon as we have the will, a moment would be enough for justice to be done.
(Peter Kropotkin, *Words of a Rebel*, p. 63)

Anarchist violence is the only violence that is justifiable ...
(Errico Malatesta, *The Anarchist Revolution*, p. 82)

How do anarchists think they will realize anarchy? This chapter considers some of the options. It begins with a discussion of the central tenet of anarchist strategies for change: that oppression can be overcome only by the free action of the oppressed. The main body of the chapter looks at the ways in which anarchists have translated this idea into different strategies, some revolutionary and some dissenting. Notable examples of strategies in the first group are propaganda by the deed, the general strike and guerrilla warfare. In addition, some anarchists – for instance, social anarchists – have adopted an evolutionary view of revolutionary change, to develop a strategy sometimes referred to as practical anarchism. Anarchists have expressed dissent through different forms of protest: from symbolic action, to direct action and civil disobedience. The discussion shows how, in recent years, anarchists have developed new and innovative ways of using these forms of protest in mass anti-globalization actions, moving away from the notion of strategic change to one of tactical reform.

Anarchist strategies of change have been the cause of serious dispute in the anarchist movement. Anarchist violence and, in particular, the relationship between anarchism and terrorism has been a subject of intense debate and remains one of the most important cleavages dividing anarchists. This issue is examined at the end of the chapter.

emancipation from oppression by the oppressed

The idea that oppression can be overcome only by the action of the oppressed is not a specifically anarchist principle. Yet in the late nineteenth century anarchists put their stamp on the idea by saddling it to a principle of direct or economic action. In this period direct action was contrasted with the rejection of (i) electoral strategies designed to sweep socialist parties to legislative power and (ii) vanguardism, the doctrine of revolutionary elitism linked to Lenin and Bolshevism.

Proudhon had floated the idea that 'the proletariat must emancipate itself without the help of the government' as early as 1848 (though in the same year he also successfully stood for election to the French Constituent Assembly). The principle was enshrined in the preamble to the statutes of the IWMA and was supported by a broad range of socialist opinion. It became a bone of contention only in the early 1870s, at the point when the International disintegrated. Then, laying the foundations of what became the division of socialists into anarchist and non-anarchist groups, Bakunin identified himself with the policy of the IWMA in an effort to discredit Marx. Marx, he argued, did not support emancipation by the action of the workers themselves – on the contrary, he believed that 'the conquest of political power' was 'the first task of the proletariat'.[1] In Bakunin's mind, these two ideas were incompatible. Others shared his view. In 1872, at a meeting in St Imier, Switzerland, anti-authoritarians reinforced Bakunin's policy distinction by voicing their disapproval with Marx's decision of 1871 to support the formation of working-class political parties. They argued that a uniform policy of revolution – that is, of political conquest – must not be imposed on the workers; that liberation could be won only by the spontaneous action of the workers; and that revolutionary action

must be taken directly against the exploiters through the expropriation of property. Whereas those who supported Marx believed that
the workers could, through their representatives, wrest control of the
state to achieve liberation, those who followed the nascent anarchist
position believed that direct action by the workers held the key to
emancipation.

By the time that working class or socialist parties began to appear
at the end of the nineteenth century, political action was identified
specifically with parliamentarism. Parliamentarism described the
electoral strategy favoured by Engels and modelled by the German
Social Democratic Party (SPD). It was soon taken up by groups
across Europe and became the official policy of the Second
International. For anarchists like Malatesta the policy was fundamentally flawed and would 'only lead the masses back to slavery'.[2]
Many non-anarchist socialists rejected the implication of Malatesta's
view, namely, that participation in parliamentary politics implied a
rejection of revolution from below. But for anarchists like Malatesta
there was a dichotomy between popular revolution and parliamentary politics. Landauer shared this view: '[t]he chief aims of Social
Democracy consist in catering for votes ... Genuine Socialist
propaganda, agitation against private property and all exploitation
and oppression is out of the question ...'.[3]

The anarchist rejection of parliamentarism, which came to a
head in the Second International, turned on a number of points. In
the 1890s Charlotte Wilson outlined the three principle anarchist
complaints.

1. The organization of political parties was authoritarian. By seeking to take power in government, socialist parties were attempt-
   ing to take command. (Chinese anarchists – following Bakunin –
   raised a more specific complaint. Not only did parliamentarism
   suggest a desire to command, it also suggested that command
   would be assumed by or on behalf of a tiny section of the workers
   – the urban, industrial proletariat – and that it would be
   exercised against the interests of the rural masses).[4]
2. Party politics was elitist: the 'lofty ideal of the socialized state
   appeals to the moral sense of the thoughtful few', but not apparently to the masses who 'supply both the dynamic force and the
   raw material essential to ... social reconstruction'.
3. Socialist parties would inevitably get bogged down in the mire of
   political competition.

... the man who wins is he with the loudest voice, the readiest flow of words, the quickest wit and most self-assertive personality. Immediately it becomes the business of the minor personalities to drag him down, as the old struggle for place and power repeats itself with the socialistic societies themselves.[5]

With the success of the parliamentary strategy and the entry of socialists into state legislatures, anarchists reinforced these complaints. One was that the comforts of office were corrupting and that parliamentary politics encouraged reformism. Emma Goldman developed this critique in the light of the success of American women's suffrage campaign. Against the claim that women could improve the quality of public life by their participation, she argued that women would be swallowed up by the system. It was a mistake, she argued, to think that the corruptness of politics was a question of 'morals, or the laxity of morals'. Politics was 'the reflex of the business and industrial world, the mottos of which are: "To take is more blessed than to give"; "buy cheap and sell dear"; "one soiled hand washes the other"'. Women could no more emancipate themselves through participation in party politics than working men; their entry into parliamentary legislatures would end in their own corruption, not the reform of the system. Moreover the scope of parliamentary politics was simply too narrow to enable women to tackle the real causes of their oppression: the hypocritical conventions that constrained them and inhibited their emotional development. For as long as women clung to the mistaken belief that parliamentary action was making a difference they would be deflected from the real task of emancipation. Consequently, Goldman concluded: 'woman is confronted with the necessity of emancipating herself from emancipation'.[6]

Traditionally, the anarchist critique of parliamentarism has extended from the refusal to participate in electoral politics to the boycotting of elections. Today some modern anarchists are willing to relax the strict prohibition on the boycotting of elections, pointing out that abstention can advantage repressive movements. Whilst the main thrust of anarchism is directed against electoral activity, anarchists like John Clark argue there is some scope in modern democracies for anarchists to vote tactically, particularly in referenda and local elections.

Unlike parliamentarism, vanguardism provides no space for compromise. The anarchist concern with vanguardism as a form of political action was stimulated by the rise of Leninism and the success of the Bolshevik revolutionary strategies. Otto Rühle's critique of Bolshevism described this concept (which Lenin elaborated in his 1902 pamphlet *What is To Be Done?*) in the following terms:

> The party was considered the war academy of professional revolutionists. Its outstanding pedagogical requirements were unconditional leader authority, rigid centralism, iron discipline, conformity, militancy, and sacrifice of personality for party interests. What Lenin actually developed was an elite of intellectuals, a centre which, when thrown into the revolution would capture leadership and assume power.

On this account vanguardism represents a dramatic return to Marx's policy of political action – one that blatantly contradicts the principle of worker emancipation. Indeed, Rühle argued that vanguardism was posited on a belief that the workers were incapable of emancipating themselves. The Russian revolution, he noted, provided an excellent opportunity for the workers to take direct control of the revolutionary process through the organization of the soviets. Yet the actions of the workers were frustrated largely because Lenin failed to

> … understand the real importance of the soviet movement for the socialist orientation of society. He never learned to know the prerequisites for the freeing of the workers. Authority, leadership, force, exerted on one side, and organization, cadres, subordination on the other side … Discipline and dictatorship are the words which are most frequent in his writings … he could not comprehend, not appreciate … what was most obvious and most … necessary for the revolutionary struggle for socialism, namely that the workers once and for all take their fate in their own hands.[7]

The positive strategies that anarchists have developed for worker-emancipation do not reject the possibility of education or the co-ordination of revolutionary actions. Early on Bakunin argued that the success of the revolution and, indeed, any collective action, turned on 'a certain kind of discipline'. He also believed that agents organized in secret, fraternal associations ('brotherhoods') could play a valuable role in encouraging and helping the masses in revolutionary situations: '[o]ne hundred revolutionaries, strongly and earnestly allied, would suffice for the international organisation in the whole of Europe. Two, three hundred revolutionaries will suffice for the organisation of the greatest country'.[8] He even argued that these agents might exercise a 'collective dictatorship' in the process of revolution. Yet just as he distinguished natural authority from state authority, he drew a line between his understanding of discipline/dictatorship and the statist ideas he associated with Marx. Anarchist discipline, he argued, was 'not automatic but voluntary and intelligently understood'. And when it came to dictatorship, Bakunin noted:

> This dictatorship is free from all self-interest, vanity, and ambition for it is anonymous, invisible, and does not give advantage or honour, or official recognition of power to a member of the group or to the groups themselves. It does not threaten the people because it is free from official character. It is not placed above the people like state power because its whole aim ... consists of the fullest realisation of the liberty of the people.[9]

Malatesta endorsed Bakunin's position. The masses, he argued, were perfectly capable of rebelling against their oppressors, but they lacked technical skill and they needed '[m]en, groups and parties ... who are joined by free agreement, under oath of secrecy and provided with the necessary means to create the network of speedy communications' to help them secure victory. These men were not a vanguard since their 'special mission' was to act as 'vigilant custodians of freedom, against all aspirants to power and against the possible tyranny of the majority'.[10]

Modern activists talk in terms of affinity groups rather than brotherhoods. The Spanish Iberian Anarchist Federation (FAI) – an organization of anarchist militants who worked within the CNT – has provided the model for this form of organization. Affinity groups bring activists together on the basis of friendship in small, fluid autonomous groups to ferment revolution in the wider population. Membership might be very small, and meetings informal. However the group is more than a debating society or drinking circle. As Guérin explained, affinity groups act as 'an ideologically conscious minority' to enlighten the masses and combat the reformist tendencies of other worker or protest organizations. Something akin to this model was adopted by the Angry Brigade, a group of anarchists engaged during the 1960s in a high-profile campaign against the British state. But this idea of organization appeals to a wide spectrum of anarchist opinion, from social anarchists involved in community networking schemes to class struggle anarchists.

Some anarchists still feel uneasy with this form of organization and argue that the premises on which it is based are inherently elitist. One anti-capitalist protester has put the point thus:

> For all that activist cells and secret societies have long been part of the revolutionary tradition, they are deeply problematic for anarchism. While Leninists and authoritarians of all descriptions have no problems with decisions being made by an elite minority, a central tenet of anarchism is that decisions should be made by the people affected by them. That kind of democratic control is ruled out if the movement, or the anarchist part of it, goes underground – we'll be left with small groups doing what they think is in everyone's interests, instead of everyone getting a chance to make their own decisions.[11]

Proponents of revolutionary organization respond that there is a difference in principle between Bakuninism and Leninism. Stuart Christie's defence is based on the Bakuninist idea that anonymity protects anarchists against a 'vainglorious' slide into vanguardism. The Angry Brigade, he argues, 'remained anonymous. It made no bid or claim to leadership'.[12] The London-based Anarchist Federation (AF) argue by assertion: their aim is to establish 'semi-secretive (but never elitist) non-permanent "workplace resistance" groups' of dedicated revolutionaries – 'anti-capitalist, anti-company, anti-union and anti-party political'.[13] Alfredo Bonanno's more robust defence is posited on the openness of affinity groups to non-anarchists, the avoidance of 'generic' programmes for change and, above all, the autonomy of groups from political parties and trade union organizations. The 'organizational logic' of what is called insurrectional anarchism is towards permanent conflict, not towards the creation of new forms of administration or control.

Whether or not anarchists should organize agitation groups to foster mass insurrection remains a moot point. All three major insurrectionary strategies that anarchists have devised provide space for such action. These are propaganda by the deed, the general strike and guerrilla warfare. Even practical anarchism, a non-insurrectionary strategy, is consistent with affinity group organization.

revolutionary strategies

propaganda by the deed

This strategy had its origins in 1877 when it was used by Malatesta and comrades to provoke a peasant insurrection in Benevento, near Naples. The idea behind the principle was that small bands of dedicated revolutionaries would stir up revolution by inciting peasants. In Italy revolutionaries moved

> ... about in the countryside as long as possible, preaching war, inciting to social brigandage, occupying the small communes and then leaving them after having performed there those revolutionary acts that were possible and advancing to those localities where our presence would be manifested most usefully.[14]

The most notable act of propaganda by the deed was the destruction of land registry documents. In spirit the policy was Bakuninist. Bakunin's strategy called for the destruction of all political, judicial, civil, and military institutions by the non-payment of taxes, rents and debts and the refusal of conscription. Yet propaganda by the deed was not endorsed as a revolutionary strategy until the 1881 London Anarchist Conference. Here it was understood to justify any act, legal or otherwise, from the production and distribution of underground propaganda to political violence. Kropotkin's *An Appeal to the Young* captured the essence of the idea and was printed in several European languages by socialists of all hues. In 1898 the English anarchist David Nicoll presented a more graphic illustration in his translation of Kropotkin's *The Spirit of Revolt*:

> ... from ... peaceable reasonings to insurrection and revolt there is an abyss, that which, with the greater part of humanity, separates the *argument* from the *deed*, the *thought* from the *will*, the desire to act.
>
> How has this abyss been crossed? ...
>
> The reply is easy. It is the action of minorities ... Courage, devotion, the spirit of self-sacrifice ...
>
> What form will this agitation take? The most varied forms which are dictated by circumstance, means, temperaments. Sometimes gloomy, sometimes lively ... but always audacious; sometimes collective, sometimes purely individual ...[15]

Propaganda by the deed has very negative connotations. One reason for this is that the strategy was modelled on an assumption of violent insurrection and civil war. In Bakunin's hands this idea of revolution received its most darkly romantic treatment. Bakunin defined revolution as a heroic, cathartic act. It was for those with 'blood in their veins, brains in their heads, energy in their hearts' and he celebrated the revolution's *spontaneous, uncompromising, passionate, anarchic and destructive* character. Bakunin also embraced the prospect of civil war because it was 'always favourable to the awakening of popular initiative'. It 'shakes the masses out of their sheepish state … breaks through the brutalizing monotony of men's daily existence, and arrests that mechanistic routine which robs them of creative thought'.[16] Later-nineteenth-century anarchists tended to write more in expectation of revolution than with foreboding, but shared Bakunin's romanticism. In 1882 Reclus declared that '[i]n spirit the revolution is ready; it is already thought – it is already willed; it only remains to realize it'.[17] And Malatesta spoke for many others when he argued:

> We are revolutionaries because we believe that only the revolution, the violent revolution, can solve the social question … We believe furthermore that the revolution is an act of will – the will of individuals and of the masses; that it needs for its success certain objective conditions, but that it does not happen of necessity, inevitably, through the single action of economic and political forces.[18]

Propaganda by the deed was not incompatible with propaganda by the word, but in the minds of its proponents its strength was its ability to provoke a final, speedy, cataclysmic revolutionary event, not its power to educate. Many anarchists denounced this vision as repellent and/or misguided. The tradition extending back to Proudhon was to consider revolution in pacific terms, as the triumph of the principle of association and free contract over the chaos of state control, or the victory of the ego over the social order that sought to repress it. Notwithstanding Proudhon's often militant rhetoric, anarchists in this tradition despaired of Malatesta's vision of barricades, mines, bombs and fires. Indeed, the English anarchist Henry Seymour argued that the rejection of insurrectionary violence was an ideological test that helped distinguish anarchist individualism from communist anarchism.

Whilst Proudhonians rejected the idea of insurrection, many more anarchists were repelled by the terrorism associated with propaganda by the deed. In the late 1880s and '90s propaganda by the deed came to be associated exclusively with individual acts of terrorism. At first, European anarchists, particularly in France – and later those in the Americas, the US and Argentina – assassinated or attempted to assassinate numerous heads of state and business leaders; some targeted ordinary bourgeois. Killings were accomplished with knives, guns and, most terrifying of all, explosives. In this guise propaganda by the deed gave rise to a cycle of violence in which the often heavy-handed responses of states to anarchist outrages or the threat thereof encouraged new cohorts of anarchists to become dynamiters and assassins in protest. More pointedly, it led to the killing or execution of a number of anarchists without evidence of wrong-doing: the Haymarket Martyrs and Sacco and Vanzetti were the most celebrated cases (Pino Pinelli – the model for Dario Fo's play, *The Accidental Death of an Anarchist* – is a well-known modern-day anarchist martyr).

Propaganda by the deed is often discussed as a strategy that had relevance only in the nineteenth century. And the thrust of much modern anarchism is towards non-insurrectionary forms of revolutionary action. John Clark develops a widely held view that anarchist change is primarily a matter of altering 'consciousness and character'.[19] For some anarchists the task is educational. As one Australian group argues: the 'job for revolutionaries is not to take up the gun but to engage in the long, hard work of publicizing an understanding of this society'.[20] For others, it's regenerative. In the late 1960s Roel Van Duyn developed an idea of 'level-headed agitation'. If individuals wanted anarchy, each would have to learn how to become less like a citizen and more like a 'kabouter', fantastic gnome or pixie, able to combine the contradictory attributes of the 'urbagrarian', the 'resident nomad' the 'practical theorist, intellectual gardener [and] altruistic egoist'.[21]

Yet not all anarchists have distanced themselves from the idea of insurrection. Bookchin turns to events like the Spanish revolution and the May-June upheaval in Paris of 1968 to find a paradigm for anarchist change. He rejects Clark's critique of the insurrectionary model of revolution as an attempt to replace 'left-libertarian politics with poetry and mysticism' and a hopeless collapse into 'social-democratic' gradualism.[22] Alfredo Bonanno develops an idea of insurrection as 'armed joy': a spontaneous explosion of passionate rebelliousness directed against the 'death' and 'insanity' of the commodity spectacle. He quotes the early-nineteenth-century utopian revolutionary Dejacque: 'Forward everyone! And with arms and heart, word and pen, dagger and gun, irony and curse, theft, poisoning and arson, lets make ... war on society'.[23] Zerzan too revels in the potential violence of insurrection, sharing Bookchin's enthusiasm for the Paris uprising and treating events like the 1992 Los Angeles riots as markers of insurrection. He also embraces terrorism as revolutionary instrument, celebrating the Unabomber for establishing a clean break with armchair rebellion:

> Enter the Unabomber and a new line is being drawn. This time the bohemian schiz-fluxers, Green yuppies, hobbyist anarcho-journalists, condescending organizers of the poor, hip nihilo-aesthetes and all the other 'anarchists' who thought their pretentious pastimes would go on unchallenged indefinitely – well, it's time to pick which side you're on ...
>
> Some, no doubt, would prefer to wait for a perfect victim. Many would like to unlearn what they know of the invasive and unchallenged violence generated everywhere by the prevailing order – in order to condemn the Unabomber's counter-terror.
>
> But here is this person and the challenge before us.
>
> Anarchists! One more effort if you would be enemies of this long nightmare![24]

Whilst notions of insurrection endure in the anarchist movement, many anarchists argue that the success of revolution depends on the extent to which anarchists can extend their influence amongst the workers and use insurrection as a platform for construction. The syndicalist alternative is to bring about revolution through general strike.

the general strike

Like propaganda by the deed the origins of the general strike are sometimes traced to Bakunin. Whilst developing his ideas of revolutionary fraternity, Bakunin considered the ways in which the masses might be educated to understand the causes and cures for their oppression. Instruction was one method, but in Bakunin's view, education or propaganda were by themselves inadequate tools to move the oppressed to rebellion. Another way 'for the workers to learn theory is through practice: *emancipation through practical action*'. This required the 'full solidarity of the workers in their struggle against their bosses, through the *trade unions and the building up of resistance*.[25] Anarcho-syndicalists like Ferdinand Pelloutier and Rudolf Rocker took Bakunin's idea to elaborate a full-blown revolutionary strategy.

The role of syndicates is to defend the interests of producers within capitalism in a manner that challenges reformism. Workers are encouraged to develop a sense of unity and are equipped with the technical skills and economic knowledge necessary for them to take direct control of production in the event of revolution. The principle of syndicalist struggle is direct action. Direct action is sometimes understood to mean purely industrial action without the intermediary of trade union officials. However, Rocker offered a tighter definition. In accordance with the principle of emancipation, direct action described action taken through 'the instruments of economic power which the working class has at its command'. But it also described actions that were designed to provoke a response from the state.[26]

Syndicalists employ a number of tactics to further their aims, notably sabotage, boycott and occupation. In addition, they use slowdowns, the work-to-rule, the sitdown or 'quicky strike' and the sick-in (in which workers spontaneously develop illnesses which prevent them from working). Max Nettlau argued that one of the most effective weapons of syndicalist action is the good work strike, where workers shoulder responsibility for their labour and refuse to undertake work which compromises its quality. On such an action, builders might 'resolve that no unionist may touch slums – helping neither to erect nor to repair them'. Nettlau believed that this kind of action was truly revolutionary: if London builders decided to refuse work on slums 'by one stroke the question not only of housing but also of landlordism would come to the front. The cry of the public in reply would be *No Rent*! And the shop assistants might help by coming out, refusing to handle further the abominable food which they now sell'.[27]

Critics of anarcho-syndicalism – from Malatesta to Bookchin and Bonanno – argue that labour organizations are more likely to protect or improve the position of their members in the existing system than they are to work for revolutionary change. This should not prevent anarchists from taking part in labour movement struggles, but should alert them to the fact that syndicates cannot be regarded as *anarchist* organizations. They also argue that syndicalist structures tend to ossify, undermining the ability of grass-roots members to take initiatives and encouraging syndicalist leaders to issue directives from above. Committed anarcho-syndicalists reject these claims and argue that the syndicalists' chief weapon, the strike, provides a perfect medium through which to realize their goals.

The idea of early-twentieth-century anarcho-syndicalists was that local wildcat strikes would culminate in a general strike of all workers and that this would demonstrate both their immense power whilst simultaneously provoking a reaction from government and the employers that would provide the spark to civil war and popular rebellion. The self-consciously utopian picture described by Emile Pataud and Emile Pouget suggested that:

> The most obvious result of the repressive efforts of the capitalists was to make the breach between them and the working class deeper and wider. Things had come to such a pass, that periods of calm were now rare.
>
> When the crisis lessened in one Union, it became envenomed in another. Strikes followed strikes; lock-outs were replied to by boycotts; sabotage was employed with ruinous intensity.
>
> This happened to such an extent, that there were manufacturers and commercial people who came to regard their privileged position as a not very enviable one, and even doubted its being tenable.[28]

In reality, the general strike has not proved to be such a decisive weapon. Strikes have succeeded in frightening the authorities, in demonstrating the significant power and resolve of the workers and in achieving particular aims. But the general strike has failed to sustain momentum for revolution. The limited success of anarcho-syndicalist action suggests that if the general strike is to be employed as an instrument of revolution, it must be both strong enough to withstand violent repression and sufficiently well-organized to begin self-management. The danger of the general strike is that it collapses either into reformism or into armed struggle. This is what one recent scenario suggests:

> … we are ready to use every form of dissuasion in the course of the struggle – particularly the destruction of machines, stocks and hostages to get the state forces in retreat and disarmed. At a less acute stage in the struggle, there would be point in cutting off water, gas, electricity and fuel for active bourgeois districts, to dump refuse on them, to sabotage lifts in blocks of flats etc.

... As soon as possible, factory machinery is converted for a rapid
armaments programme, ...

For immediate use, we could use piping transformed into
rocket-spear tubes. Air rifles, catapults for grenades and molotov
cocktails, flame-throwers, mortars, ultra-sonic generators, lasers ...
We can also study different sorts of armouring for converting lorries
and bulldozers, bullet-proof jackets, gas masks, antidotes to
incapacitants, the use of L.S.D. in the water supply of
enemies etc ... .[29]

In this scenario the general strike becomes indistinguishable from
guerrilla warfare.

guerrilla warfare

Anarchists usually credit Nestor Makhno with developing guerrilla
warfare as a revolutionary strategy. Makhno operated between
1918–21 in the South Ukraine, fighting in turn, German and
Austrian armies of occupation, General Denikin's White Russian
forces and, finally, the Bolshevik Red Army. His battle was waged in
defence of the spontaneous rural rebellion sparked off by the
Russian Revolution. Anarchists had long argued that the peasantry
were an inherently revolutionary force. Indeed, Bakunin had
defended the idea of the rural jacquerie, accusing Marx of wanting to
swallow up the 'peasant rabble' in an urban workers' state. Landauer
argued a similar case. Socialists, he argued, 'cannot avoid the struggle
against landownership. *The struggle for socialism is a struggle for the
land; the social question is an agrarian question*'.[30] Makhno followed
this tradition. He believed that the peasantry's 'innate' impulse was
to anarchism. In 1917 'the toiling masses' had transferred 'the land
confiscated from the great landlords and the clergy to those who
worked it or ... intended to do so without exploitation of another
man's labour'. They would gravitate naturally towards the organization of producer and consumer co-operatives based on free
association in communes. His role was to protect the peasants'
revolutionary gains and to extend the process of revolution by
spreading propaganda. Makhno's version of guerrilla action was as
much about communication as it was about fighting. And though
Voline believed that the movement lacked sufficient intellectual
force, Makhno organized a Commission for Propaganda and
Education in the Insurgent Army.

At first Makhno organized small military units that could move rapidly across the countryside, forcibly expropriating the landed aristocracy and the bourgeoisie. According to Voline, the Makhnovists were as 'swift as the wind, intrepid, pitiless towards their enemies'. They would fall 'thunderously on some estate', massacre 'all the sworn enemies of the peasants' and disappear 'as rapidly as they had come'.[31] This activity was an intimate part of the struggle. For Makhno it was 'only through that struggle for freedom, equality and solidarity that you will reach an understanding of anarchism'.

In the longer term, Makhno's experience of the civil war in the Ukraine led him to conclude that success in guerrilla warfare depended on the creation of a tighter revolutionary structure. At the height of the civil war he proposed the formal organization of the guerrilla army. Instead of recruiting all volunteers to free battalions, he suggested vetting recruits to weed out potential traitors. He also insisted that recruits maintain 'fraternal' or 'freely accepted discipline'. As Voline explained, rules of discipline 'drawn up by commissions of insurgents ... [and] approved by general assemblies of the various units ... had to be rigorously observed'. Finally, Makhno advocated the division of fighters into well-defined units to be 'coordinated by a common operational Staff'.

Some anarchists have argued that Makhno's strategy has a general application. For example, Daniel Guérin treated the Makhnovist struggle as 'a prototype of an independent mass peasant movement' and a precursor of guerrilla actions in China, Cuba, Algeria and Vietnam. More recently, anarchists like Zerzan have found evidence for the potential of the strategy in the Mexican Zapatista movement. Other anarchists believe that something like Makhnovism can be applied in urban environments. The model for this idea – guerrillaism – comes from organizations active in the 1960s and '70s like the Weather Underground (in America), the Tupamaros (Uruguay), the Red Army Faction and the Red Brigades (Germany and Italy). In this context, guerrilla action is not so much a means of waging revolutionary war as an instrument for the preparation and provocation of revolutionary action. As the Red Army Faction put the point: urban guerrillaism is premised on the idea that 'by the time the moment for armed struggle arrives, it will already be too late to start preparing for it'.[32]

Yet the lessons of guerrilla warfare and, more particularly, urban guerrillaism, are not clear-cut. One problem is that assumptions of the would-be guerrillas are often crudely macho. Web-based advice on the construction of pipe-bombs, rockets and short-range mortar, comes with the warning that '[w]andering away to have a fling with a local babe ... could result in getting oneself and the entire group killed'.[33] Critics argue that such attitudes betray something of the inherent authoritarianism of guerrilla warfare and its incompatibility with anarchist principles.

These suspicions have been fuelled by the tendency of guerrilla movements to emerge from Marxist-Leninist rather than anarchist stables. The Red Army Faction and the Red Brigades are well-known examples. Notwithstanding the enthusiasm of writers like Zerzan, some anarchists fear that the Zapatistas might prove to be another and question the leadership role assumed by the media-savvy Subcomandante Insurgente Marcos. In cases where the motivations of the guerrillas are not in doubt, anarchists warn that guerrilla action suits would-be commanders as well as it suits anarchists. As Stuart Christie argues, the Cuban revolution gave the Marxist Fidel Castro the edge over his anarchist-leaning rival, Camilo Cienfuegos.

In the Makhnovist struggle, the argument about the appropriateness of guerrilla action to secure revolution was played out in the context of Makhno's reforms of the militia and his proposals, made in exile in the 1920s, that revolutionaries establish a General Union of anarchists to direct revolutionary and political activity. His conviction was that anarchists would forever fail in revolution unless they accepted the necessity of wielding armed revolutionary power. Indeed, he believed that the anarchists' inattentiveness to revolutionary discipline explained their failure to counter Bolshevism. Having once incited the masses 'to join in the struggle' anarchist forces were incapable 'of marshalling ... resources against the revolution's enemies'. Makhno was extremely sensitive to the charge that this organizational framework represented a betrayal of anarchist principles. But his response was firm:

> Anarchism is and remains a revolutionary social movement and that is why I am and always will be an advocate of its having a well articulated organization and support the establishment, come the revolution, of battalions, regiments, brigades and divisions designed to amalgamate, at certain times, into one common army, under a single regional command in the shape of a supervisory organizational Staffs. The task of the latter will be, according to the requirements and conditions of the struggle, to draw up a federative

operational plan, co-ordinating the actions of regional armies, so as to bring to a successful conclusion the fighting conducted on all fronts against the armed counter-revolution.[34]

Makhno's critics were not convinced. Malatesta attacked the proposal to create an anarchist union, arguing that it sounded too much like a defence of revolutionary government.[35] Voline criticized Makhno's militarism. In his view 'any army, of whatever kind it may be, always and inevitably ends by being affected by certain serious faults, by a special kind of evil mentality'.[36] Similar arguments about military organization were rehearsed in Spain. Admittedly, in the Spanish context, the issue was complicated and embittered by the enforced militarization of the anarchist militias under Stalinist control. Nevertheless, the war seemed to pose Spanish anarchists with a similar problem to the Makhnovists: to fight a campaign of heroic indiscipline or one of hierarchical efficiency.

Some anarchists believe that Makhno misstated the problem facing revolutionaries. The question was not how to organize a guerrilla army, but how to fight a guerrilla war. Advocates of guerrilla action argue that guerrilla warfare does not demand militarization or specialization. Indeed, reflecting on the defeat of the Spanish revolution Peirats defended the principle of guerrilla warfare precisely because it offered anarchists an opportunity to struggle in a manner that was consistent with their principles. The lesson of the revolution, he argued, was that the anarchists should have organized themselves more like the Mahknovists had done prior to the formal militarization of the insurgent army. The revolution failed not because of militarization as such, but because anarchists adopted a strategy that made militarization more or less inevitable. They wrongly attempted to fight a trench war. The failure to consider the possibility of 'civil war by organizing support bases for guerrilla actions in the countryside and the mountains' played straight into the hands of the enemy.[37] The strength of guerrilla warfare, he argued, is its potential to confront the enemy on terms that revolutionaries are best equipped to fight. Peirats believed that the guerrilla warfare demanded organization, but it was of a qualitatively different kind from that suggested by Makhno: the success of the strategy depended on the establishment of strong links between urban and rural areas and the development of reliable supply systems and bases for guerrilla training. For as long as anarchists did not enjoin their enemies in formal battle, they could avoid the need to organize in

Anarchist insurrection: summary

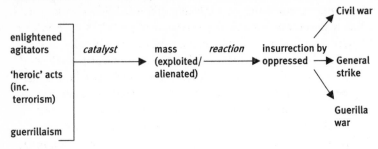

formal or perhaps in regimented military units and consequently improve the chances of revolutionary success. Australian anarchists echo Peirats' point:

> … in certain conditions, as in peasant-based societies, it would be necessary to set up armed bases in the country-side. But the aim here would not be to carry out "exemplary" clashes with the military but to protect the political infrastructure to enable the spreading of ideas to continue. This may involve some guerrilla tactics but it cannot mean a strategy of guerrillaism. Nor can it mean the creation of a separate, hierarchical, military organization, which is not only anti-libertarian but is also vulnerable and inefficient.[38]

Anarchists might never be sure that guerrilla leaders will not develop a taste for power. But Peirats' defence suggests that guerrilla war can be waged in a manner that is consistent with anarchist aims.

practical anarchism

The leading insight of practical anarchism is that revolution can be achieved by evolutionary means. The strategy, which is associated with writers like Colin Ward and Paul Goodman, is designed to bring anarchism into everyday life. Ward argues that the strategy – which he calls anarchy in action – is 'an updating footnote to Kropotkin's *Mutual Aid*'. In other words, it is an attempt to show that anarchy is a current in our everyday lives and that the job of the anarchist is to help individuals and groups to express their natural tendencies.

The primary difference between this and other anarchist strategies for revolution is that it does not demand a final rupture with the state in the form of civil war or insurrection. Ward's anarchism has never worked on the basis of this assumption. For others, however, the adoption of practical anarchism represented a change in view. During the Second World War British anarchists like Herbert Read thought that the 'war would inevitably lead to revolution – that it would be neither won nor lost without social upheaval'. By the end of the War, he called on comrades to 'repent their mistake' and admit '[t]here will be no revolution – just yet'.[39] By the 1960s anarchists who accepted this judgement identified the evolutionary aspect of practical anarchism as its chief advantage over competitors. For example, George Woodcock recommended the strategy because it was non-violent and because it represented a break from the romantic utopianism of 'old anarchism'. Against the 'bellicose barricaders' of the 1940s he argued:

> The kind of mass movement at whose head Bakunin challenged Marx in the First International, and which reached its apogee in the Spanish CNT, has not reappeared … Except for a few dedicated militants, anarchists no longer tend to see the future in terms of conflagratory insurrection that will destroy the state and all the establishments of authority and will immediately usher in the free society … Instead of preparing for an apocalyptic revolution, contemporary anarchists tend to be concerned far more with trying to create, in society as it is, the infrastructure of a better and freer society.[40]

Woodcock believed that practical anarchism was relatively unambitious. The strategy was not designed to create 'an anarchist utopia' but a more participatory, less bureaucratic, more decentralized and open society. Yet for Ward the strategy is no less revolutionary than the insurrectionary doctrines it replaces. Indeed, in his view, the commitment to create a self-organizing society, 'a network of autonomous free associations for the satisfaction of human needs', is a struggle against capitalism, bureaucracy and monopoly and it 'inevitably makes anarchists advocates of social revolution'.[41] Paul Goodman argued that practical anarchism had a utopian aspect and that it was radical in its focus, if not its scope. Its proposals appeared to be 'simple-minded' but they forced individuals who felt well-off and at ease in democratic society to confront their real powerlessness in the face of capitalist production and the increasingly complex social systems that controlled their lives.[42] The idea was to create an environment in which these people could recreate themselves as fully rounded, equal citizens.

The emphasis of Ward's anarchism is organizational and he is as interested in finding evidence of anarchist experimentation as he is to show how anarchy might flourish. For example, he shows how groups of people have co-operated to look after their housing needs in the face of bureaucratic indifference or hostility. He considers the ways in which peoples have looked after their own health needs outside the framework of the state; how they have used unemployment as a platform to establish alternative economies and the success with which co-operatives have managed local transport systems and neighbourhood services, from schools to radio-stations. In contrast, Goodman's concern was with the psychological condition of Western societies and, rather than looking for evidence of anarchy in everyday life, he considered how ordinary institutions and environments might be reformed to encourage the expression of personality. His view was that modern capitalism produced personnel much in the same way as it produced other consumer goods. The quality of human life had been impoverished as a result.

Although their approaches to practical anarchism differ, both Ward and Goodman identified two particular strategic interests: education and urban planning. Their concern with education is that in Western societies schools bred disaffection whilst failing to address significant social and economic inequalities. Contrary to popular belief, Goodman argued, in America 'the poor youth ... will not become equal by ... going to middle-class schools'.[43] And the reason why not is that education is used exclusively as a means of sorting children into achievement groups. It fails to develop potential or build imagination, sympathy and trust. It fails even to address the socio-economic and cultural factors that affect achievement. In response to the concern of government with educational standards Ward argues '[a]s the threshold of competence rises, so the pool of inadequacy widens'. Far from providing a route to social advancement – still less equality – education supports a cycle of inequality. Ward quotes the sociologist Michael Young: '[t]oday you have to be far smarter to get by, and if you are not, we penalise your children'.[44]

Goodman developed a six-point plan to correct contemporary 'miseducation':

1. Use school less. Children, he argued, 'will make up the first seven years school-work with four to seven months of good teaching'.
2. Educate outside the classroom. This proposal was not new. Kropotkin's scheme for integrated education included the

recommendation that children learn geography, for example, by examining the physical world. Goodman urged teachers to 'use the city ... its streets, cafeterias, stores, movies, museums, parks and factories' as sites for education. Children learned far better from experience than they did through abstraction.

3. Bring non-teachers into school: 'the druggist, the storekeeper, the mechanic' to break down the barriers between the school and the adult world.

4. Abolish compulsory attendance. The model here was A.S. Neill's Summerhill, a progressive school in which pupils attended lessons voluntarily.

5. Build small school units, equipped with 'a record-player and pin-ball machine', to allow children to integrate work and play in a friendly environment.

6. Send children out of school to farms for 'a couple of months a year'. For as long as 'the farmer [fed] them and not beat them', farm visits would help children to think of alternatives to urban living.[45]

Ward and Goodman approached urban planning as they approached education: with a view to finding ways of overcoming alienation and providing a context for co-operation. One of Ward's inspirations is *Fields, Factories and Workshops*, Kropotkin's attempt to show how agriculture and industry can be integrated to provide a basis for local self-sufficiency and decentralized systems of production and consumption.[46] Ward denies that he is necessarily fixed to the idea of 'small is beautiful' and believes that practical anarchism can be made to operate in the context of consumer society. His idea is not to rebuild the environment but to use planning and architecture as tools that allow individuals and communities to continue with their anarchist experiments in social living. Thus planning is something that should be wrested from the control of government and put in the hands of those responsive to the needs of dwellers and users.

In *Communitas*, a book which Ward describes as 'one of the most stimulating of the last century', Goodman outlines his ideas of city planning. The book, originally published in 1947, ends with a master plan for the re-development of Manhatten. The purpose of the plan is to make New York 'a city of neighbourhoods wonderful to live in, as leisurely and comfortable as it is busy and exciting'. It involved using the waterways and developing the shores of the Island as 'beaches for bathing, boating and promenade', and developing park and recreational space to 'restore leisure to a place that is notorious for its nervousness'. Goodman confines business and industry mostly to a central strip running up the Island and flanked by two major highways. Central Park disappears but residences are built in the extended parkland areas stretching out beyond these arterial roads.[47] In a revised plan, Goodman proposed banning traffic altogether in New York City.

The appeal of Goodman and Ward's work is its ability to integrate anarchist projects 'within the world of the practically possible'.[48] This approach has inspired a younger generation of anarchists to similarly engage in lived experience and to provide support and advice to those seeking practical routes to emancipation. Yet Goodman and Ward admit that there is an inherent conservatism in their strategy. Goodman endorsed the ideas of Edmund Burke, the eighteenth-century philosopher and so-called father of conservatism, to the effect that the legitimacy of government turned on its ability to protect community. His work was an attempt to restore a condition of life he believed capitalism and the modern state had undermined. For his part, Ward acknowledges that there is a certain similarity between his ideas of mutual aid and those propounded by writers like David Green, who embrace self-help as a means to improve 'consumer control' of public services.[49] Moreover, in the context of the capitalist welfare state both also acknowledge the obstacles to their strategy. Goodman claimed that his ideas were 'common sense' but that they also made people 'feel foolish and timid'. And he could not show how or why individuals would be persuaded to make the changes that would allow them to overcome their psychological repression. Ward's answer, that individuals are in the process of making these changes and that they have only to adopt the best practices highlighted in his work, runs up against the realities of state provision. Ward admits that there is a problem:

> The positive feature of welfare legislation is that contrary to the capitalist ethic, it is a testament to human solidarity. The negative feature is precisely that it is an arm of the state. I continually find myself quoting the conclusion of Kropotkin in *Modern Science and Anarchism* that 'the economic and political liberation of man will have to create new forms for its expression in life, instead of those established by the State' and that 'we will be compelled to find new forms of organisation for the social functions that the state fulfils through the bureaucracy'.[50]

Over a hundred years since Kropotkin there is little sign that people feel compelled to seek alternatives to the services offered by the bureaucratic state. And though Ward is probably right that practical anarchism is more attractive to more people than strategies that promise revolution and civil war, it runs the risk of encouraging would-be anarchists to judge 'what should be' by the standards of 'what is'.

protest

The difference between protest and revolution used to be one of expectation: anarchists protested when they believed that there was little potential for revolution and in the hope that the protest would increase it. Now, some new anarchists – particularly those influenced by postmodern and poststructuralist ideas – see protest as the only legitimate form of revolutionary action. On the first view, protest provides a means of mobilizing peoples and, by provoking counteraction, of illustrating the truly repressive character of authority. On the second, it is not directed towards the removal or replacement of constituted power, but towards the expression and development of plural ways of acting. For both, however, it is possible to distinguish four categories of protest: constitutional action, symbolic action, direct action and civil disobedience. This section examines these forms of protest and then considers the ways in which anti-globalizers have employed them as instruments of mass protest.

constitutional action

Constitutional action describes orthodox, legal forms of protest. Owing to their denunciation of representative or parliamentary democracy anarchists are not usually associated with this form of action. Yet anarchists make good use of the legal framework and the liberal freedoms of speech, press and association it provides to produce books, leaflets and journals, organize public meetings, lecture series, summer schools, conferences and discussion groups. Today the internet provides anarchists with perhaps the most effective means of constitutional action – even primitivists who despise technology are well organized on the web.[51]

Most constitutional action is directed towards education and the publication of anarchist ideas. In the hands of groups like the Guerrilla Girls, it is also used as an instrument of cultural subversion. By organizing workshops and producing posters, freely available on the web, the group reveal the male norms embedded in modern culture – and in particular in the Hollywood film industry – and probe the relationship between masculinity, power and violence. Constitutional action is also used as a critical tool. In their pamphlet 'What's Wrong with McDonald's?' London Greenpeace asked readers 'to think for a moment about what lies behind McDonald's clean, bright image' and attempted to enlighten them with the facts. In 1990 the McDonald's corporation disputed the factual basis of London Greenpeace's claims in what became known as the McLibel trial – the longest libel trial in English judicial history. But in doing so they unwittingly underlined the power of constitutional action to fulfil a strong propaganda role.

symbolic action

Symbolic action consists of 'those acts that aim to raise awareness of an issue or injustice, but by themselves do not attempt to resolve it'. Symbolic acts are those that 'signify other acts'.[52] April Carter suggests that symbolic actions are designed to 'create solidarity and confidence', pointing to vigils and marches, fasts, slogans and songs as examples of symbolic acts.[53] More recently, Lindsay Hart has distinguished between two main forms of symbolic action: 'bearing witness' and 'obstruction'. The first, which has a long history in the Quaker movement, is designed to tap the public's conscience. By attending incidents or sites of injustice, protestors aim to exploit media coverage to raise awareness of abuse and provoke outrage at its continuation. This form of protest has been employed by groups from the Clamshell Alliance – an association of American anti-nuclear protestors in New Hampshire – to those involved in the International Solidarity Movement who draw attention to acts of violence and degradation committed by Israeli forces in the Palestinian Occupied Territories. The second is widely employed to prevent road building, tree clearing, the movement of traffic and of arms and it demands of activists that they use their bodies to block unjust or oppressive actions – locking-on (to heavy machinery, transport, etc.) or sitting down in front of trains, tanks and bulldozers.[54]

Symbolic action is often undertaken in the spirit of purposeless purpose. Activists take heart from Mahatma Gandhi: '[w]hatever you do will be insignificant, but it is very important that you do it'. Others argue that symbolic action offers a particularly good way of playfully subverting cultural norms and of ridiculing accepted standards. The execution of a statue of Christ by Spanish anarchists organized in a firing squad in the early months of the civil war is one example of an action at once 'absurd and glorious'.[55] The attempt made in the early 1990s by London anarchists to levitate the Houses of Parliament was another. Goaman and Dodson cite activities like the London underground party and the proposal for a 'Blatant Fare-Dodging Day' by the Fare Dodgers' Liberation Organisation.[56] Other symbolic actions include 'prayers to the product' – Sunday worship organized outside stores like Diesel in chichi areas such as London's Covent Garden – and 'reverse theft': stocking stores with useable items recovered from refuse.

The emphasis on building solidarity and protesting without hope of success lends symbolic action an essentially innocent air. Yet symbolic action can be provocative and aggressive. A general strike can be a symbolic act. Vernon Richards defended terrorism as a symbolic act. The well-targeted assassination of a dictator or tyrant, he argued, might not secure tangible reform, but could still reverberate positively around the world, boost the morale of the oppressed and send a powerful message to the oppressors.[57] Less obviously provocative symbolic acts can have equally profound effects. As Rudolf de Jong notes, the slogan coined in the 1960s by the Provos (Dutch anarchists) 'the police is our dearest friend' unexpectedly raised the ire of the authorities and helped create an atmosphere of tension, distrust and civil unrest.[58]

direct action

Carter and Franks agree that the concept of direct action has been used so indiscriminately – particularly by the media – that it is now almost meaningless. The confusion surrounding the term is probably due to the range of different activities the action supports. Yet there are two defining characteristics of direct action. First, it's about empowerment, 'about breaking from dependency on others to run our lives'. It is action taken 'not indirectly by "mediators" or "representatives" ... but directly by those affected'. Second, it is 'action intended to succeed, not just to gain publicity'.[59] As Franks argues, it describes an act intended to present 'a partial or temporary solution to a larger set of practices'. David Wieck offers this definition:

> If a butcher weighs one's meat with his thumb on the scale, one may complain about it and tell him he is a bandit who robs the poor, and if he persists and one does nothing else, this is *mere talk*; one may call the Department of Weights and Measures, and this is *indirect action*; or one may, talk failing, insist on weighing one's own meat, bring along a scale to check the butcher's weight, take one's business somewhere else, help open a co-operative store, etc., and these are *direct actions*.[60]

Direct action is often associated with illegality and sometimes criminality. Since the nineteenth century anarchists have been known to support acts of simple theft – not only in the shape of fare dodging, but in the guise of bank robbery and shoplifting – as a legitimate part of anarchist campaigning. To the distress of anarchists like Guérin, the Bonnot Gang (usually credited with having thought of the idea of the getaway car before Bonnie and Clyde) firmly linked French anarchism to banditry. In Australia, the outlaw Ned Kelly achieved a similar feat, now often celebrated as a progenitor of homegrown anarchism. Yet because direct action is designed to solve a problem and because anarchists have difficulty showing how mere criminality fits this bill, it usually has an overtly 'political' character, even if it is illegal.

Whilst direct actions are intended to move beyond symbolism, they may have a symbolic element. To give an example: in the 1960s anarchist anti-Francoists used small bomb attacks in their campaigns. Their actions symbolized a desire to topple the regime, but were intended to have a direct effect on would-be holiday-makers, creating fear whilst avoiding harm, and on the tourist industry that helped legitimize Franco's rule. Squatting is probably the best-known and most widely practised form of direct action, and one that anarchists are keen to encourage. Squatting can be used to further experiments in community living and as a form of protest. In the first sense, it is a form of practical anarchy, associated both with the problem of homelessness and the creation of alternative forms of community – co-operatives or, more recently, co-housing projects, where groups of people living in private residences share kitchen, laundry, workshop and child care facilities. As a form of protest squatting has recently been used by eco-anarchists. One example

was the Pure Genius squat, set up in 1996 on a patch of derelict land
owned by Guinness in Wandsworth, South London. The squat was
turned into an 'eco-village', permanently inhabited by between 50 to
100 people. Pure Genius could neither resolve the shortage of
housing in London nor remedy the ecological damage sustained by
the city, and to this extent the protest was symbolic. Yet the squat
raised these issues through the press interest it generated; and to the
extent that the squatters demonstrated the possibility of an alternative way of life, it was a practical response to a particular situation.

Sabotage is a well-known form of direct action, once pioneered
by syndicalists and now assuming new forms. One is 'hactivism' or
cyber activism. It includes the jamming or infiltration of computer
systems and the subversive use of domain names to attack well-
known corporate brands: Starbucks is a favourite. Another form of
sabotage is monkeywrenching. Monkeywrenching is particularly
associated with eco-anarchists and it describes a form of non-violent
direct action. Unlike traditional saboteurs who attempted to clog up
production processes, monkeywrenchers 'act heroically in defence of
the wild to put a monkeywrench into the gears of the machine that is
destroying natural diversity'. This 'safe, easy, fun, and ... effective'
activity includes tree spiking, the disabling of road-building equipment and the sinking of whalers.[61] Back in the towns, anarchists
encourage urban climbing and wall protests, 'unreality TV' –
performance for CCTV cameras – and culture jamming through
subvertising or adbusting – the defacing, reshaping and overpasting
of billboards to challenge corporate gloss. A sales pitch for Rover
simply reading 'Enjoy', was subverted with the addition of: 'more
pollution'. To give another example, an advert for a Hyundai
miniature which read 'Amuse the kids, Park it sideways in the garage'
was subvertised with 'and leave it there'. Advertising hoardings are
not subvertiser's only targets. Creative use of green felt pens to
highlight and transform the 'buck' in 'Starbuck' and the 'off' in
'coffee house' helps to take some of the shine from the corporate
logo. Other anarchists create spoof ads: one idea for vodka pictures
a name-tagged foot in a morgue with the slogan 'Absolute on Ice'
underneath. Following a similar logic, anarchists produce placards
urging 'bomb poor people', 'bombs not bread', 'money is my life'.
Reclaim the Streets (RTS) have pioneered the street party as a form
of direct action against the car, consumerism and segmentation of
public life. The action involves whole neighbourhoods, thus
drawing new audiences to the campaign whilst simultaneously

helping to revive local community networks. RTS argue that these illegal actions often wrong-foot the authorities because they emphasize the extent to which anarchism fosters collective responsibility, communality and fun. Whilst some class-struggle anarchists denounce RTS campaigning as middle-class posturing, others point out that RTS actions have mobilized effective mass support for old-style workers' struggles.

civil disobedience

Civil disobedience is usually defined as an act of non-violent resistance (even in the face of violence) to a specific injustice for which participants anticipate arrest. The definition distinguishes civil disobedience from direct action: a monkeywrencher who attempts to disable bulldozers covertly wherever they are found is engaged in direct action, whilst a monkeywrencher who commits the same act publicly and in order to frustrate a particular building scheme is performing an act of civil disobedience. Like symbolic and direct action it is popular with non-anarchist as well as anarchist protestors. However, in contrast to non-anarchist civil disobedience, anarchist civil disobedience does not imply an acknowledgment of the state's legitimacy. To the contrary, anarchists disobey with the long-term commitment to its overthrow (some anarchists prefer the term 'social' to 'civil' disobedience in order to emphasize this difference).

Civil disobedience is associated with four particular writers and activists – Thoreau, Tolstoy, Gandhi and Martin Luther King – and takes two forms. For followers of Thoreau civil disobedience can take violent or non-violent forms. In 1859 Thoreau famously defended the murder of five unarmed pro-slavery settlers by the abolitionist John Brown as an act of civil disobedience. In Thoreau's view, each individual should decide what constitutes appropriate action. In contrast, Tolstoy, Gandhi and King rejected violence. Indeed, Tolstoy not only believed that violence was immoral, he specifically rejected the appeal to conscience as a justification for anarchist terrorism. There was, he believed, an intimate relationship between the means and ends of revolutionary change such that an act of violence was more likely to perpetuate than overcome an injustice based on the exercise of violence. Gandhi adopted a similar view. One of the outstanding features of his Sarvodaya movement was that means are never instrumental, but always end-creating.[62]

These two forms of civil disobedience are sometimes confused. For example, whilst Franks argues that civil disobedience is distinguished by what he calls its strong consequentialism (i.e. those engaging in civil disobedience work towards a particular end and justify the action through its attainment) he runs this idea together with a fundamental commitment to non-violence. His premise allows the possibility for violence, but his conclusion is Tolstoyan. The confusion stems in part from the habit of libertarians – Rand is one – to equate civil disobedience with non-coercive action, on the grounds that it is based on an appeal to individual conscience, not mass protest. Alternatively, activists involved in Peoples' Global Action (PGA) suggest that the confusion rests in the concept of 'non-violence'. This idea, they contend, is ambiguous and interpreted in culturally specific and sometimes contradictory ways. The differences are particularly marked in Europe and India. In view of this confusion, the PGA no longer include a commitment to 'non-violence' in their Hallmarks and activists are instead encouraged to seek ways of confronting oppression by considering the suitability of specific actions in the prevailing local conditions. In other cases, the ambiguity reflects a deliberate attempt to push a policy of non-violence. George Woodcock presents the assumption of non-violence as a fundamental principle of civil disobedience. Indeed, he so downplays the differences between Thoreau's position and that of the other writers that one could be forgiven for thinking that civil disobedience was informed by a unified tradition of thought.

For all the confusion, anarchists have interpreted civil disobedience in both senses. For example, Zerzan's idea of resistance is closer to Thoreau's than Tolstoy's. Denying that questions of resistance turn on violence or non-violence, he argues that the primary consideration informing action is individual conscience. Consequently, his personal conviction that 'words are a better weapon to bring down the system than a gun would be' carries no implications for 'anybody else's choice of weapon'.[63] His willingness to defend the Unabomber's choice is very much in the spirit of Thoreau's defence of Captain Brown.

Probably more anarchists have equated civil disobedience with the Tolstoyan view. The strength of the commitment owes something to the causes with which the action has been associated. In the post-war period, civil disobedience was the preferred tactic of peace activists and campaigners against atomic and nuclear arms. For many of the anarchists involved in these campaigns, the commitment to non-violence was central to the oppositional stance they wished to take. The popularity of Bart de Ligt's 1937 guide to war resistance, *The Conquest of Violence*,[64] helped to seal the association between the struggle for peace and non-violent protest. His argument was that warmongering was neither effectively nor legitimately combatted by war-like behaviour. Developing this logic, anarchist peace protestors argued that non-violent civil disobedience was a perfect match for anarchism. Alan Lovell, an anarchist member of the Committee of 100 (the organization founded in 1960 from within the British Campaign for Nuclear Disarmament) argued that Gandhian non-violence 'was something new'. It broke the fantasy of exercising state power and stemmed 'from a different attitude to politics ... more relevant ... than Marx'. The 'whole question of non-violent civil disobedience', he argued, 'is very closely tied up with decentralisation'.[65] In a similar vein, Derrick Pike defines 'anarcho-pacifism' as an organizational response to Bakuninism:

> The anarcho-pacifists ... want to use an entirely different method to produce the social revolution ... Anarcho-pacifists will never use violence to make others change their ideas and behaviour; instead they make clear what kind of society is best for everybody, and they persuade others to share their philosophy ... they do not need to have any secret communications or clandestine meetings. Always they are overt, not covert. When there are enough anarcho-pacifists, we will all start living in a free society.[66]

The argument between pacifists and their opponents has never been resolved and it has implications for all forms of anarchist protest, not just civil disobedience. In recent times, the debate has been conducted within the anti-globalization movement.

anarchism and anti-globalization

The anti-globalization movement is not a specifically anarchist phenomenon. However, anarchists involved in the movement believe that the mass protests like the Battle for Seattle in December 1999 (when protestors succeeded in shutting down the meeting of the World Trade Organization), and the Genoa summit of the G8 in July 2001 (when over-zealous policing resulted in the death of Carlo Guiliani) have given them an almost unparalleled opportunity to extend the influence of their ideas. They have been encouraged in this belief by the apparent 'unconscious' anarchism of the movement: both the appeal that decentralist and anti-hierarchical principles exercise across the movement as a whole, notwithstanding its plurality, and the unity of action demonstrated by activists. As Naomi Klein argues, there is a general consensus within the anti-globalization movement that 'building community based decision-making power – whether through unions, neighbourhoods, farms, villages, anarchist collectives or aboriginal self-government – is essential to countering the might of multinational corporations'.[67] Whilst new social movements, non-governmental organizations and political parties channel these ideas to state agencies, anarchist anti-globalizers contend that the mobilization of popular opinion against neo-liberal corporate economics is the movement's greatest strength. For them, the anti-globalization movement has opened up a new sphere of democratic participation and, through this participation, it has drawn ordinary citizens across the globe into anarchistic action. The promise of the anti-globalization movement is that it avoids the 'staging' and 'workerism' of syndicalist strike actions and extends beyond the sprayings, brickings, glueings and bombings undertaken by disparate 'guerrilla' groups. The challenge of the anti-globalization movement is to discover how to translate intuitive anarchistic practice into anarchist action.

Peace activists in the 1960s confronted a similar problem. Then, advocates of non-violent civil disobedience argued that the protest movement had a revolutionary potential, but that protestors needed to be drawn into a wider campaign of direct action. Anarchists disagreed about how they should release this potential. Some argued for programmes of practical anarchy, others for more aggressive strategies, shaped by affinity groups. Alan Lovell's hope was that protest would bring about gradual social change: 'you gain power over *this* institution, you change *that* one, you put a bit of pressure *here*'. In time, he argued, 'there is a change, so that people have much more control over their lives, control which they have actually taken themselves'.[68] Similarly, in 1964 Robert Swann argued that the peace movement was 'equipped by the way of organisation, motivation, and understanding' to accomplish lasting anarchist change and that they 'should include in their agenda ... a constructive programme for *revitalization of the cities*'.[69] On the other side of the argument, Vernon Richards argued that the peace movement had succeeded in convincing 'many thousands of people ... to participate in "illegal" demonstrations' but it was an illusion to suppose that 'the violence of our existing social system can be destroyed by massive non-violent demonstrations'.[70] The way forward was to combine practical programmes with strike actions and permanent rebellion.

Militants in the anti-globalization movement tend not to see the parallel between their predicament and that faced by the '60s activists. Indeed, many accounts suggest that the campaign for peace has a different dynamic from the anti-globalization move-ment. Whereas the former was idealistic and passively engaged in anarchist struggle, the latter is and actively engaged.

Anarchists active in the anti-globalization movement undertake a full range of protest actions. Some are involved in labour organiza-tions, others prefer what are called 'fluffy' or non-violent forms of symbolic protest ('Tactical Frivolity'). As a participant in Genoa describes, anarchists in this group wear pink and silver, dress up as fairies, are inspired by the vision of 'a massive global party full of happy loving rocking tick tockin' fun and funky free people living in peace, laughing singing dancing and playing like they've never played before'.[71] Less fluffy Wombles (White Overalls Movement Building Libertarian Effective Struggles) invert symbols of violence by dressing in foam and paper protective gear and organize a range of confrontational activities – from samba parties and lockdown blockades to illegal camps and squats and the occupation of public transport. At the 'spikier' end of the spectrum, anarchists join the Black Bloc, a loosely organized black-clad cluster of affinity groups and individuals, distinguished by their commitment to violence – as a means to resist arrest, assist in 'un-arrests', break police lines and meet state violence head-on. Elements within the Black Bloc are also committed to property damage, some targeting symbols of multi-national power and sweat-shop production – financial institutions, Nike and Levi stores, Starbucks and McDonald's – others undertaking the indiscriminate destruction of shops, cars, bus shelters, telephone kiosks, and other public buildings and utilities.

These forms of action appear to have little in common. Yet militants consider that there is more that binds these direct actions together than there is to tie any one of them to the peace protests of the past. As one militant puts it, 'the fact that [actions] … haven't involved ritualistic wandering up and down through city streets has given people a reason for taking part'. The lesson, he continues,

… is that if the protest revert to ritualistic walking up and down, if they are seen to be something of a waste of time, a lot of … people are likely to stay at home. The challenge therefore is to find a way to keep people involved, to find a way in which the tactics used are seen to be effective and therefore attract the maximum number of people to participate in whatever protests are held. Furthermore, it is necessary to look for ways to establish structures which will allow for maximum participation in discussions as to what these tactics should be.[72]

Unlike the '60s generation, who started from a common platform of non-violent protest and then argued about the appropriateness of this strategy for the development of an anarchist movement, anarchist anti-globalizers now embed and demonstrate their preferred approaches to the problem of translation through the particular actions they adopt. Moreover, through this commitment to active engagement, they argue that the diversity of actions highlights the solidarity of the movement, its plurality and willingness 'to openly discuss' differences and mistakes and its eagerness to avoid getting 'tied down by the baggage of ideology'. In the words of one group:

Meaningful action, for revolutionaries, is whatever increases the confidence, the autonomy, the initiative, the participation, the solidarity, the egalitarian tendencies and the self-activity of the working class, and whatever assists in their demystification. Sterile and harmful activity is whatever reinforces the passivity of the working classes, their apathy, their cynicism, their differentiation through hierarchy, their alienation, their reliance on others to do things for them and the degree to which they can therefore be manipulated – even by those allegedly acting on their behalf.[73]

Unfortunately, whilst mass protests have attracted media attention and raised issues of global oppression in public arenas, there is little evidence to suggest that they have enjoyed any greater success in building alternative sites of revolutionary activity than the 'passive' peace protests spearheaded by campaigners like Lovell. Indeed, anarchists involved in networks like PGA have voiced concerns that militants have failed to build sufficiently strong links between mass actions and local grass roots activities, leaving protestors cut adrift at the end of protests. Similarly, whilst plans for mass actions continue apace, some militants argue that the tactics adopted at these mass demonstrations might be more usefully employed in smaller arenas against specific targets – military installations, corporate meetings, and so forth.

Yet the suggestion that the anti-globalization movement has pioneered a novel form of anarchistic action points to an important difference between it and the older peace campaigns, namely, the politicization of protest. Unlike the earlier generation of anarchists – who had significant moral and political disagreements about strategy – modern activists enter into protest with the idea that their protests offer a route to anarchy or at least serve as a statement of intent. Actions are about cultural subversion, building solidarity, debate and the destruction of corporate power. Whatever kind of actions militants take – fluffy or spiky – they reflect ideological commitment. The Beltane 2000 Communiqué issued by the Comrades of Kaczynski Group is written in post-Situationist prose and leans towards primitivism, but is infused with the spirit of much modern protest:

> Fellow revolutionaries, come, walk with us in the moonlight, let the darkness blur the division between all forms of life and reclaim our wildness. We are quickly becoming feral, and thus we are more fed up with civilization and any forces that wish to maintain this disintegrating status quo …
>
> Insurrection exists on the boundaries of every assumption. In the words of the situationists, we will ask for nothing, we will demand nothing; we will take, we will occupy. Stop asking for freedom from the very people who have made the word necessary by separating us from the wild. In every action taken, we will never be satisfied with anything less than a full collapse. No more half-assed reformist band-aids. Those who fight and settle for petty reform are as much our enemy [as] those who enforce law … A community garden is insurrection. Free coffee on the sidewalk is insurrection. A letter-bomb is insurrection. Settle for nothing less! [74]

This conviction provides the context for recent debates about anarchism and violence.

anarchism and violence

Since the emergence of propaganda by the deed in the late nineteenth century, debates about anarchist revolution have often focused on the question of violence. Anarchists have usually positioned themselves in the resulting debates by distinguishing revolutionary violence from terrorism. The table below gives an indication of where leading anarchists stand.

Anarchist positions on violence and terrorism

Revolution	Violence	Terrorism	
Likely/necessary	Unnecessary/unjustified	Justified	Immoral/ineffective
Bakunin, Kropotkin, Malatesta, Reclus, Makhno, Goldman, Richards, Bookchin, Zerzan	Proudhon, Tolstoy, Woodcock, Clark, Ward	Reclus, Malatesta, Richards, Zerzan	Kropotkin, Tolstoy, Goldman, Bookchin, Clark, Woodcock, Ward

There are significant differences between these positions, even between those anarchists who fall in the same broad group. Debates between anarchists have centred on two particular issues: justification and explanation. Though the arguments are complex, it is possible to delineate some of the main lines of debate through the discussions of the Black Bloc.

Anarchist responses to property damage perpetrated by the Black Bloc are both moral and pragmatic. Looking first at the critical case, the moral argument is that violence attracts a certain kind of authoritarian personality. Some writers simply describe members of the Black Bloc as hooligans and delinquents: 'anarkids' not anarchists. Their desire to commit violence is an indication of their urge to dominate and oppress. A variant on this theme is that even sincere militants are driven to authoritarianism through violence. Echoing discussions of Makhnovism and guerrillaism, some critics of the Black Bloc argue that property destruction encourages spikies to think in terms of militarization. One militant complains about a proposal to elect certain individuals and affinity groups to 'tactical facilitation units' from within the Black Bloc and to give these units 'command' positions.

The pragmatic case has three parts. First, critics argue that property damage is largely pointless and that whilst 'there's something to be said for blowing off steam', those who engage in property destruction are more interested in dressing up 'in gas masks and bandanas' than they are in weighing up its usefulness as a

revolutionary tactic. Second, violence breeds repression. A fluffy
analyst of the anti-globalization protests argues that anarchists who
commit violence have fallen into a trap. The authorities, she argues,

> … want to make us out to be terrorists to give them the go ahead to
> squash our global and strong movement. This is the same propa-
> ganda they use to start wars, they frighten people into believing we
> are evil terrorists. Be careful: our actions could put the whole
> movement in danger … Cop bashing, however much of a buzz at
> the time and a great point scorer, doesn't save the world and is a
> distraction. It is also the distraction the real terrorists, the government
> want from us.[75]

Third, there is concern that the authorities can exploit the commitment to violence to their own advantage. One worry is that incite-
ments to violence can degenerate into the 'ranting of the frustrated'
and lead to 'unnecessary arrests and mistakes'. Another is that
groups practising violence are open to infiltration from police.
Police forces have for many years used *agents provocateurs* to entrap
unwary anarchists and to involve them in phoney plots which
undermine the movement by creating dissent, distrust and suspicion.
In the nineteenth century, police engaged in all manner of covert
activities – French police even set up their own anarchist newspaper.
The fear of infiltration remains strong. Of course, all manner of
anarchist groups (particularly since 9/11) attract the attention of the
authorities and are open to infiltration, whether or not they support
violence. In the course of the McLibel trial, London Greenpeace
discovered that at least seven spies were employed by McDonald's or
Special Branch to monitor the group, often attending more meetings
than genuine anarchists and sometimes outnumbering them. Yet the
possibility that police might infiltrate groups committed to violence
carries more serious consequences than infiltration elsewhere since
success can result in the movement being saddled with responsibility
for the most outrageous atrocities. Critics charge the Black Bloc
with leaving anarchism particularly vulnerable to this sort of
police attack.

Both the moral and the pragmatic critiques have found a ready
response. The 'moral' defence of violence relies on a relativist argument about anarchist and state violence. Jason McQuinn develops
this point. Responding to pacifist critics of the Black Bloc from
within the anti-globalization movement, he argues:

So who are always the first people to call out to those who protest to 'Stop the Violence!'? Is it the people who are being assaulted and beaten by cops, gassed with chemical weapons, shot with 'non-lethal' as well as deadly weapons? The people who are suffering the brunt of the violence? Of course not. This call almost always comes from those who support the great mass of violence that is always aimed at the protestors by the police, their provocateurs and other government-controlled armed forces.[76]

The pragmatic defences are that violence is purposeful, that it does not have undesirable consequences and that it is necessary. For example, responding to the claim made by 'the peace police' that anarchist violence is mere hooliganism, the ACME collective deny that they 'are a bunch of angry adolescent boys'. Property destruction 'is not merely macho rabble-rousing or testosterone-laden angst release. Nor is it displaced and reactionary anger. It is strategically and specifically targeted direct action against corporate interests'. Trashing businesses is the 'next best thing' to transforming social spaces into 'places of "public dialogue"', looting and rioting the 'most ready-to-hand assertion of our collective power'.[77] Against the claim that anarchist violence breeds repression, militants argue that there is no direct link between the two. More than one eye-witness account of the action in Genoa suggests that the authorities did not neutrally defend property. Even those involved in the 'colourful, pacific, fluffy' street theatre were 'attacked by the police, with water cannon and tear gas'. The ACME Collective's response is similar:

> ... tear-gassing, pepper-spraying and the shooting of rubber bullets all began before black blocs ... started engaging in property destruction ... we must resist the tendency to establish a causal relationship between police repression and protest in any form, whether it involved property destruction or not. The police are charged with protecting the interests of the wealthy few and blame for the violence cannot be placed upon those who protest those interests.[78]

Finally, violence is a necessary part of anarchist transformation. Turning from property damage to terrorism, the Unabomber, Ted Kaczynski, presses the case. Anticipating the collapse of the 'techno-industrial system' Kaczynski warns that 'the "bourgeois" types – the engineers, business executives, bureaucrats' represent the most potent threat to the revolution – not just the military officers and police. They 'won't hesitate to use force and violence when these are necessary for their achievement of their objectives'. Anarchists must also be prepared to defend themselves 'physically against these people'.[79]

Anarchists and observers of anarchism tend to be less divided in their explanations of violence than in their attitude towards its justification. The leading argument is that violence is motivated by noble intentions – this is the 'good terrorist' argument (after Doris Lessing's novel). Individuals commit violence largely because they feel compelled to do something about the oppression and exploitation they see around them. In 1969 Bruce McSheehy argued that the commitment to violent action – which he believed endemic to anarchism – was intimately connected to the anarchists' desire to remove those fetters that inhibited the masses from expressing their innate capacity for self-government.[80] In 1971 Michael Lerner advanced a similar case: violence was central to American countercultural anarchism; it was an expression of the anarchists' identification with outcasts and criminals and a reflection of their desire to recover 'the capacity for love'.[81] Militants do not always cast themselves as latter-day outlaws or idealists. Nevertheless, they sometimes explain their adoption of violence with reference to the state's oppression. Similarly Stuart Christie writes:

> My conscious choice about the manner of my involvement in the anti-Francoist resistance was as a fighter – as opposed to being a helper of Franco's victims. To do otherwise would have felt like running away, psychologically and intellectually. I would have felt hypocritical choosing the easy and safe – but useless and ineffective – options of demonstrations, picketing and leafleting and not challenging Franco head on, as it were.
>
> Feeling as strongly as I did about his regime, [how could I] claim exemption from the struggle and stand aside from the moral imperative of challenging that which I strongly felt to be wrong? Seeing someone injured and doing nothing to help is to act negatively; as granny said, 'we are not bystanders to life'.[82]

Marxist critics sometimes argue that these explanations suggest that anarchists are damaged, deluded characters, tilting at windmills and driven by emotion rather than rationality. For the historian Eric Hobsbawm, it is no coincidence that Spain, the land of Don Quixote, was an anarchist stronghold. Yet at the heart of the good terrorist explanation is an idea of responsibility and private judgement. Rather than seeing individuals as, for example, bearers of class (proletarian or bourgeois), anarchists argue that individuals can choose to work for or against revolutionary change. This idea of choice is common to anarchists as different in outlook as Tolstoy and Zerzan, Bakunin and Ward, class struggle anarchists and primitivists. Naturally, taking responsibility is not equivalent to a commitment to violence. Helen Steel, one of the defendants in the McLibel trial, described her motivation to get involved in London Greenpeace in much the same way as Christie explained his decision to fight Franco: '[I]f I see oppression it's just like a gut feeling that I want to do something to challenge it and change it and end it ...'.[83] But her campaign was constitutional. Jon Purkis also understands responsibility in a wholly non-violent way, combining an individualist concern with lifestyle choices with a communitarian willingness to build and sustain self-organized and non-exploitative public utilities.[84] However, if violence is considered to be purposeful – as activists in the Black Bloc contend – responsibility suggests that the question anarchists should ask themselves is not whether they should be prepared to use aggression against the state or civilization, but how and when they should do so.

summary

This chapter has looked at a variety of anarchist strategies for change, both insurrectionary and evolutionary. It has also examined the way in which anarchists have employed different methods of protest to promote their causes. It is sometimes suggested that anarchists lack viable means of change and that the weakness of their strategies can be estimated by their failure to realize anarchy. This criticism seems to misstate the relationship between the means and the ends of the anarchist revolution and to underestimate the problems facing the anarchists whilst underplaying their achievements. The aim of anarchist revolution is to bring about emancipation from oppression by the oppressed. The difficulty that anarchists confront is not just how to find a way of defeating their enemies so that anarchy might flourish but to enthuse individuals to liberate themselves. In this second task, they have not failed and however disappointing their historic and heroic defeats, the anarchists are surely right to evaluate revolutionary strategies by their potential to deviate from the goal of self-emancipation, not merely by their effectiveness to defeat state power.

Anarchists remain divided about how best they promote anarchist action and one of the issues that most divides opinion is the use of violence. Yet none of the responses anarchists give to the issue of violence suggests that anarchist action is motivated by irrationality or a messianic devotion to a cult of destruction. Anarchists have developed their strategies for change in particular historic and political conditions in order to meet complex sets of ideas about the nature and purpose of anarchist goals.

further reading

Luigi Fabbri, *Bourgeois Influences on Anarchism* (Tucson: Sharp Press, 2001)

Graham Chesters, Jon Purkis and Ian Welsh, 'Not Complicated, but Complex', *Anarchist Studies*, 12 (1), 2004: 76–80

Karen Goaman, 'Globalisation versus Humanisation', *Anarchist Studies*, 11 (2), 2003: 150–71

Karen Goaman, 'Anarchism, Realpolitik and "Global Civil Society"', *Anarchist Studies*, 12 (1), 2004: 72–5

Peter Kropotkin, *An Appeal to the Young*, http://dwardmac.pitzer.edu/ Anarchist_Archives/kropotkin/appealtoyoung.html

Geoffrey Ostergaard, 'Resisting the Nation State: Anarchist and Pacifist Traditions', http://www.ppu.org.uk/ e_publications/ dd-trad6.html

Anton Pannekoek, *Workers' Councils* (Edinburgh: AK Press, 2003)

David Stafford, *From Anarchism to Reformism* (London: Weidenfeld & Nicholson, 1971)

J. Tracy, (ed.) *The Civil Disobedience Handbook* (San Francisco: Manic D Press)

Henry David Thoreau, *Political Writings*, (ed.) Nancy Rosenblum (Cambridge: Cambridge University Press, 1996)

Simon Tormey, *A Beginner's Guide to Anti-Capitalism* (Oxford: Oneworld, 2003)

Colin Ward, *Anarchy in Action* (London: Freedom Press, 1982)

H. Zinn, *Disobedience and Democracy* (Cambridge, Mass.: South End Press, 2002)

links

Adbusters: http://adbusters.org
Anarchist People of Color: http://www.illegalvoices.org
Activist Network: http://www.activistnetwork.org.uk/index.php
Black Bloc for Dummies: http://www.infoshop.org/blackbloc.html
Earth Liberation Front: http://earthliberationfront.com/about
Guerrilla Girls: http://www.guerrillagirls.com
International Workers' Association (IWA): http://www.SolFed.
    org.uk
Laboratory of Insurrectionary Imagination: http://www.labofii.
    net/documentation/index.html
Prayers to the Product: http://www.thevacuumcleaner.co.uk/
    prayers.html
Reclaim the Streets: http://www.reclaimthestreets.net
Save our Starbucks (SOS): http://www.starbuckscoffee.co.uk
Shifting Ground: http://www.shiftingground.org
Wombles: http://www.wombles.org.uk
Workers Solidarity Movement: http://struggle.ws/wsm.html

notes

1. M. Bakunin, *On Anarchism*, S. Dolgoff (ed.) (Montreal: Black Rose, 1980), 288.

2. E. Malatesta, *Life and Ideas*, V. Richards (ed.) (London: Freedom Press, 1977), 158.

3. G. Landauer, *Social Democracy in Germany* (London: Freedom Press, 1896(?)), 2.

4. A. Dirlik, 'The Path Not Taken: The Anarchist Alternative in Chinese Socialism, 1921–27', *International Review of Social History*, xxxiv, 1989, 1–41.

5. C. Wilson, *Three Essays on Anarchism* (Orkney: Cienfuegos Press, 1979), 13.

6. E. Goldman, *Red Emma Speaks*, A.K. Shulman (ed.) (London: Wildwood House, 1979), 135–6.

7. O. Rühle, *The Struggle Against Fascism Begins with the Struggle Against Bolshevism* (London: Elephant Editions, 1990), 11; 14.

8. A. Lehning, 'Bakunin's Conceptions of Revolutionary Organisations and Their Role: A Study of His 'Secret Societies', in C. Abramsky (ed.), *Essays in Honour of E.H. Carr* (London: Macmillan, 1974), 68.

9. Bakunin to Nechayev, M. Confino (ed.) 'Bakunin's Letter', *Encounter* 39, (1) 1972: 85.

10. Malatesta, *Life and Ideas*, V. Richards (ed.) (London: Freedom Press, 1977), 161; 164.

11. 'Bashing the Black Bloc?', *Black & Red Revolution* no. 6, 2002, http://flag.blackened.net/revolt.rbr/rbr6/black.html

12. S. Christie, *The Christie File* (Orkney: Cienfuegos Press, 1980), 228.

13. Anarchist Federation, *Beyond Resistance* (London: AF, 2003), 27.

14. J. Joll, *The Anarchists*, 2nd edn. (London: Methuen, 1979), 103.

15. D. Nicoll, *La Carmagnole: The Spirit of Revolt* (London, 1898), 4–5.

16. Bakunin, *On Anarchism*, 188; 205.

17. E. Reclus, 'Anarchy: By an Anarchist', *Contemporary Review*, XLV, 1882: 640.

18. Malatesta, *Life and Ideas*, 154

19. J. Clark, 'A Social Ecology', *Social Anarchism*, 2000, http://library.nothingness.org/articles/anar/en/display/303

20. Anarchist Communist Federation, *You Can't Blow Up a Social Relationship* (San Francisco: Acrata Press, 1985), 7.

21. R. Van Duyn, *Message of a Wise Kabouter* (London: Duckworth, 1972), 97.

22. M. Bookchin, *Whither Anarchism? A Reply to Recent Critics*, 1998, http://dwardmac.pitzer.edu/Anarchist_Archives/bookchin/whither.html

23. A. Bonanno, *Armed Joy*, 1977, http://www.geocities.com/kk_abacus/ioaa/a_joy.html

24. J. Zerzan, *Running on Emptiness* (Los Angeles: Feral House, 2002), 162.

25. Bakunin, *On Anarchism*, 167.

26. R. Rocker, *Anarcho-Syndicalism* (London: Phoenix Press, n.d.), 65.

27. M. Nettlau, *Responsibility and Solidarity in the Labor Struggle* (London: Freedom Press, 1900), 8.

28. E. Pataud and E. Pouget, *How We Shall Bring About the Revolution* (London: Pluto Press, 1990), 5.

29. Ratgeb, *ABCD of the Revolution: From Wild-Cat Strike to Self-Management in Everything* (Get It Together Yourself Books, n.d.), 6–7.

30. G. Landauer, *For Socialism* (St Louis, Missouri: Telos Press, 1978), 134.

31. Voline, *The Unknown Revolution* (Montreal: Black Rose, 1975), 559.

32. Red Army Faction, *RAF* (Edinburgh: AK Books, 1990), 22.

33. Anon., *Guerrilla Warfare: An Introduction to the Art of Revolution*, n.d., http://www.insurgentdesire.org.uk/warfare.htm

34. N. Makhno, *The Struggle Against the State and Other Essays* (Edinburgh: AK Press, 1996), 23.
35. E. Malatesta, *The Anarchist Revolution*, V. Richards (ed.) (London: Freedom Press, 1995), 93–111.
36. Voline, *Unknown Revolution*, 571.
37. J. Peirats, *Anarchists in the Spanish Revolution* (Detroit: Black & Red, 1977), 14.
38. Anarchist Communist Federation, *You Can't Blow Up a Social Relationship*, 19.
39. H. Read, *Freedom: Is It A Crime?* (London: Freedom Press Defence Committee, 1945), 6.
40. G. Woodcock, *Anarchism and Anarchists* (Kingston, Ontario: Quarry Press, 1992), 128.
41. C. Ward, *Housing: An Anarchist Approach* (London: Freedom Press, 1983), 7.
42. P. Goodman, *Utopian Essays and Practical Proposals* (New York: Vintage Books, 1962), 9.
43. P. Goodman, 'Alternatives to Miseducation' in G. Woodcock (ed.) *The Anarchist Reader* (Harmondsworth: Penguin, 1983), 276.
44. C. Ward, *Talking Anarchy*, with D. Goodway (London: Freedom Press, 2003), 93.
45. Goodman, 'Miseducation', 275–6.
46. P. Kropotkin, *Fields, Factories and Workshops* (London: Thomas Nelson & Sons, 1898).
47. P. Goodman and P. Goodman, *Communitas: Means of Livelihood and Ways of Life*, 2nd edn. (New York: Vintage Books, 1960), 227–248.
48. I. Welsh and J. Purkis, 'Redefining Anarchism for the Twenty-First Century: Some Modes Beginnings', *Anarchist Studies*, 11 (1) 2003: 10.
49. C. Ward, *Social Policy: An Anarchist Response* (London: Freedom Press, 2000), 15.
50. Ward, *Talking Anarchy*, 79.
51. J. Connor, J. Fliss, L. Fredrickson, L. Jarach, R. Leighton, M. McQuinn, J. Moore and J. Slyk, *An Open Letter on Technology and Mediation* 1999, http://www.insurgentdesire.org.uk/openletter.htm
52. B. Franks, 'The Direct Action Ethic: From 59 Upwards', *Anarchist Studies*, 11 (1), 2003: 15.
53. A. Carter, *Direct Action* (London: Housemans/Peace News, 1983), 2.
54. L. Hart, 'In Defence of Radical Direct Action: Reflections on Civil Disobedience, Sabotage and Nonviolence', in Purkis & Bowen (eds), *Twenty-First Century Anarchism* (London: Cassell, 1997), 47.
55. L. Buñuel, *My Last Breath* (London: Vintage Books, 1994), 153.

56. K. Goaman and M. Dodson, 'A Subversive current? Contemporary Anarchism Considered', in Purkis & Bowen, *Twenty-First Century Anarchism* (London: Cassell, 1997), 89.

57. V. Richards, *Violence and Anarchism: A Polemic* (London: Freedom Press, 1993), 10.

58. R. de Jong, 'Provos and Kabouters', in D. Apter & J. Joll (eds), *Anarchism Today* (London: Macmillan, 1971), 167.

59. A. MacSimóin, 'Direct Action', *Workers Solidarity*, 71, 2002, http://flag.blackened.net/revolt/wsm/ws/2002/71/direct.html

60. D. Wieck, 'The Habit of Direct Action', in Ehrlich, *Reinventing Anarchy, Again* (Edinburgh: AK Press, 1996), 375.

61. D. Foreman and B. Haywood, *Ecodefence: A Field Guide to Monkeywrenching*, 3rd edn. (California: Abbzug Press, 1993).

62. G. Ostergaard, 'Indian Anarchism: The Savodaya Movement', in Apter & Joll (eds), *Anarchism Today* (London: Macmillan, 1971), 145–64.

63. Zerzan, *Running on Emptiness*, 90.

64. B. de Ligt, *The Conquest of Violence* (London: Pluto Press, 1989 [1937]).

65. A. Lovell, P. Whannel and S. Hall, 'Direct Action?', *New Left Review*, 8, 1961, 24.

66. D. Pike, *Thoughts of an Anarcho-Pacifist* (Glastonbury, Somerset: Pike, 1992), 50.

67. N. Klein, 'Does Protest Need a Vision?' *New Statesman*, 3 July 2000.

68. A. Lovell, P. Whannel and S. Hall, 'Direct Action?', *New Left Review*, 8, 1961, 16–27.

69. R. Swann, 'Direct Action and the Urban Environment', in C. Ward, (ed.) *A Decade of Anarchy* (London: Freedom Press, 1987), 248.

70. V. Richards, *Protest Without Illusions* (London: Freedom Press, 1981), 129.

71. V. Kamura, 'Love Changes Everything', *On Fire: The Battle of Genoa and the Anti-Capitalist Movement* (London: One Off Press, 2001), 57.

72. G. Kerr, 'Where to Now? Anti-Capitalist Protest – Global and Local', *Black & Red Revolution*, 7, 2003, http://flag.blackened.net/revolt. wsm.rbr.rbr7.blackblocreply.html

73. One Off Press, *On Fire: The Battle of Genoa and the Anti-Capitalist Movement* (London: One Off Press, 2001), 140.

74. Comrades of Kaczynski Group, *Conspiracy is Unnecessary*, 2000, http://www.insurgentdesire.org.uk/conspiracy.htm

75. Kamura, *On Fire*, 59.

76. J. McQuinn, "Stop the Violence!" http://www.insurgentdesire.org.uk/ stopviolence.htm

77. BM Combustion, *You Make Plans – We Make History: Ecological Collapse, Science, The Anti-Globalisation Protests and Reclaim the Streets* (London: BM Combustion, 2002), 18.
78. ACME Collective, *N30 Black Bloc Communique*, 1999, http://ww.infoshop.org/octo/wto/blackbloc.htm
79. T. Kaczynski, 'When Non-Violence is Suicide' from *Live Wild or Die*, 8, 2001, http://www.insurgentdesire.org.uk.whennon.htm
80. B. McSheehy, 'Anarchism and Socialism', *Monthly Review*, 21 (4): 59.
81. M. Lerner, 'Anarchism and the American Counter-Culture', in J. Joll & D. Apter (eds), *Anarchism Today* (London: Methuen, 1971), 42–9.
82. S. Christie, *My Granny Made Me An Anarchist: The Christie File, part 1: 1946–64*, 2nd edn. (Hastings, East Sussex: Christie Books, 2002), 199.
83. J. Vidal, *McLibel* (London: Pan Books, 1997), 62.
84. J. Purkis, 'The Responsible Anarchist: Transport, Consumerism and the Future', in J. Purkis and J. Bowen, *Twenty-First Century Anarchism* (London: Cassell, 1997), 134–51.

concluding remarks

Studies of anarchism typically conclude with brief and often gloomy assessments about its prospects. Critics like David Miller and George Crowder acknowledge the significant contribution anarchists have made to political thought – particularly their critiques of Marxism – but still emphasize anarchism's theoretical flaws and practical shortcomings. Many anarchists – particularly those who trace the roots of the movement to Lao Tzu (Kropotkin) or Etienne de la Boetie (Rothbard) – adopt a more optimistic view. Anarchism, they argue, describes a natural impulse to rebel which is deeply embedded in the human psyche and unlikely to disappear. The history of anarchism is as old as time; it extends well beyond the appearance and collapse of the European movement (1840–1939). It may have endured long periods of quiescence, but its real history is punctuated by moments of marvellous defiance: from the Anabaptist revolt and the Leveller protests to, in modern times, the Spanish Civil War, and the events of May 1968 in Paris. From this point of view, the anti-capitalist movement is only the most recent manifestation of this struggle. On the first view, anarchism describes a particular set of concepts and ideas. On the second, it's a more protean movement.

Taken by themselves, neither view seems to capture the essence of anarchist ideology: the first is too rigid, the second too broad. Yet they both point to two popular reactions to anarchism. The first is that anarchism is a nice idea on paper, but impossible in the real world. The second is that anarchism is about permanent opposition and essentially frivolous.

The first reaction seems rather odd in the sense that it's difficult to think of any ideology that has been realized in perfect form – after all, both Marxism and liberalism have been associated with serious compromises of principle. Fascism perhaps comes closer, but few would now regard this attractive – even if it seemed so to many at the time. Gandhi's remark that Western civilization was 'a very good idea' aptly captures the difficulties of putting ideas into practice. Of course, the problem with anarchism is that in its most 'utopian' forms it seeks to dismantle the political organisation that the vast majority regard as necessary, if not also desirable. And because what anarchism represents is a far more radical challenge to the *status quo* than other ideologies, anarchist proposals tend to be judged by stricter criteria of reasonableness. Whilst anarchists have been willing to provide answers to questions about organization, security, order and well-being, it's not easy to accept their answers whilst state provision is reasonably good or at least, not openly intolerable. The difficulty facing anarchists is to persuade others to give up the devil they know for one that is almost unimaginable.

The second reaction is tied to notions of youth and romantic sacrifice. Here, the suggestion is that anarchism appeals to those without responsibilities and with the time to indulge in rebellion. Though it appears similar to anarchist ideas of youthfulness, it differs markedly from them. Whereas Voltairine de Cleyre argued that anarchism was for the young at heart and that its simplicity appealed to the child in everyone, the popular view is that anarchism is little more than a fashionable pose and that it describes a phase which most people (rightly) grow out of. The association of anarchism with romanticism also has a positive and negative variant. The positive emphasizes the commitment, idealism and heroism of anarchists, the negative, their naïve enthusiasm, intolerance and willingness to endanger others in the pursuit of their cause. Olive Garnett, the diarist and novelist, recorded the following conversation with Olive Rossetti, co-editor of the nineteenth-century London anarchist paper, *The Torch*:

Olive's conversation unknown to herself was dangerously near the ridiculous. Among other schemes they have one for the conversion of the entire British police force, so that, should there be a popular insurrection in Trafalgar Square, the police, having had their humane feelings awakened by the Anarchists, will cry 'Brothers, we had rather be bludgeoned than bludgeon in support of an unjust law, we will go in a body & resign'

> To point out that the English are *not* the French, that we *like* our
> rulers, that the country is *not* in the state of France at the time of the
> Great Revolution, that our contemplated reforms are purely social
> & can be carried out by peaceful means, has much the same effect as
> has holding out a red rag to a bull.[1]

The romantic aspect of anarchism has resonated in literature.
Bomb-throwing assassins, political oppression and the dilemmas of
revolutionary action have been explored with various degrees of
seriousness in G.K. Chesterton's *The Man Who Was Thursday*,
Joseph Conrad's *The Secret Agent* and *Under Western Eyes*, Henry
James's *Princess Casamassima*, Emile Zola's *Germinal* and, more
recently, Paul Auster's *Leviathan*. Moreover, literary images are
deeply embedded in political analyses. Treatments of Bakunin
invariably build upon a romantic impression. Indeed, his physical
image has become a metaphor for a strain in anarchist thinking.
Alexander Gray's portrait is exaggerated, but not untypical:

> Bakunin was born to become a legend. Rising above his aristocratic
> traditions, be became a revolutionary by profession, associating
> himself with anything that might be termed an insurrection or
> revolt, and ultimately developing an insensate rage for destruction.
> Years of imprisonment and years of exile in Siberia ... left him ...
> great, bearded, toothless giant, returning like a spectre from the past
> to uphold the cause of anarchism ... He remained a chaotic figure –
> chaotic in his life, chaotic in this thought, chaotic in his writings –
> thoroughly unpractical and destitute of common sense, as becomes
> an anarchist, yet with something about him of likeable but rather
> spoilt child, mingling the real with the imaginary and playing at
> make-believe conspiracies, with all the paraphernalia of codes and
> ciphers designed to be used in communication with possibly
> non-existent correspondents.[2]

The anti-capitalist movement is the most recent repository for this
interpretation of anarchist thought. Whichever forms of protest
anarchists adopt, all factions within the movement are likely to be
tarred with the same broad brush. If they are not all 'hooligans', as
Tony Blair argued prior to the July 2001 G8 meeting in Genoa,
they are still part of the 'travelling circus' he denounced at the
Gothenburg EU summit the same year.
Anarchist efforts to reject this labelling have not been successful.
And current varieties of anarchism are unlikely to shed the image of

naïve rebellion and (ultimately) purposeless action. Contemporary anarchists can hardly be accused of lacking imagination or creativity, but the emphasis that some now place on process and movement risks playing into the hands of those who would suggest that anarchists cannot achieve lasting goals: for these anarchists there are no goals. Examples of anarchistic action – like that of the Zapatistas – are inspiring to most observers, but anarchists – particularly in states governed by fraud rather than force – must eventually confront the nature of the rebellion in which they are engaged. Grass-roots movements can and do bring about meaningful change. But modern history suggests that they tend to succeed only with the connivance of states. Anarchism challenges constituted authority – even if it's organized as a samba party. It might be fun, but what will anarchists do if and when the hosts say the party's over? As Buñuel pointed out, it's one thing to be an ardent subversive and revel in the absurd, carrying out summary executions and fighting civil wars is another matter altogether.

notes

1. O. Garnett, *Tea and Anarchy! The Bloomsbury Diary of Olive Garnett 1890–1893*, ed. B. Johnson (London: Bartletts Press, 1989), 107.
2. A. Grey, *The Socialist Tradition: Moses to Lenin* (London: Longmans, Green & Co., 1946), 352.

index

Page numbers in *italic* denote tables or illustrations.

175

Barclay, Harold 15, 87, 89–90, 93–4, 97
Bellegarrigue, Anselme 5
Berkman, Alexander 9, 59
Berneri, Marie Louise 98
Biehl, Janet 78–9
Black Bloc 156, 159–60, 163
Black, Bob 5, 22, 62–3
Bolshevism 28, 32–3, 36, 59, 61, 101, 126, 129, 138, 140
Bonanno, Alfredo 5, 56, 131, 134–5
Bookchin, Murray 11, 24–5, 115
  and anthropology 87, 90–1, 97
  and democracy 114
  and insurrection 134
  and social anarchism 77–9
  and social ecology 21, 22, 37, 49, 90–1, 96
  and syndicalism 111
  and utopianism 98
Brown, L. Susan 78–9, 119
Bufe, Chaz 35, 37
Bukharin, Nikolai 33, 99
Burke, Edmund 6, 146

Camus, Albert 56
capitalism: anarcho-capitalism 25–6
  anti-capitalism 4, 26, 33, 51, 109, 131, 170, 172
  and exploitation 23, 64–6, 80, 94
  global 51–2
  and state 29–33, 51, 68
Carlson, Andrew 12–13
Carter, April 148, 149
censorship 37
centralism 28, 100–1
change: anarchist 53, 76, 125–64
  and state 31, 60
Cherkezov, Varlaam 32
Chomsky, Noam 11, 22, 25–6, 48, 52
Christian anarchism 17, 18, 20, 56, 113
Christie, Stuart 131, 140, 162
Christie, Stuart and Meltzer, Albert 37
civil disobedience 152–4, 155
civilization 23, 56, 91, 96–7
Clark, John P. 25–6, 90, 117, 128, 134
Clarke, Nicki 56, 80
class 5, 22, 37, 131, 163
  and state 29, 31–3, 51, 64

and statelessness 95
coercion 46, 58–9, 72, 95, *see also* violence
Cole, G.D.H. 5
collectivism 17–19, 20, 32, 110
Comfort, Alex 11, 34, 79
Common Wheel Collective 115
communitarianism 25, 79–80, 107, 112–20
community: intentional 112, 113–16, 118
  networking 4, 112, 116–20, 131
Comrades of Kaczynski Group 158
Confederación Nacional del Trabajo (CNT) 4, 109–12, 130, 143
consensus 114–15
conservatism 60, 146
corruption 53, 56–7, 60, 76, 80, 128
creativity 54, 56, 64, 74, 76, 94
Crowder, George 11, 170

De Cleyre, Voltairine 13, 15, 17, 20, 21, 35, 171
De Jong, Rudolf 149
De Ligt, Bart 154
Debord, Guy 23
decision-making 114–15, 155
Deleuze, Giles 22, 74
democracy 104, 114–15
dictatorship 22, 31–2, 104, 129–30
Douglas, Paul H. 47
Doyle, Kevin 111
Durruti, Buenaventura 86

eco-anarchy 104–8, 150–1
ecology, social 21–2, 49, 90–1, 96, 104–8
economies, alternative 118, 144
education 63, 69, 144–5, 148
Ehrlich, Carol 117–18
Ehrlich, Howard 116, 119–20
Eltzbacher, Paul 10–15, 16, 24, 26
Engels, Friedrich 99, 127
enragés 6–7, 28
exploitation 3, 45, 50, 66–7, 72–3, 75, 86, 127, 138, 162
  capitalist 64–6, 80, 94
  of nature 124

Fabbri, Luigi 33
family 17, 55, 70, 79, 112, 116